Governance for Collaboratives:

A Guide to Resolving Power and Conflict Issues

Governance for Collaboratives:

A Guide to Resolving Power and Conflict Issues

by

Joan M Roberts

Joan Roberts Consulting

*Dedicated to all the social change agents
trying to make the world a better place!*

ACKNOWLEDGEMENTS

Writing a book is an incredible journey. After publishing my first book, I received a great deal of positive feedback, which was very liberating. Taking the risk of putting my thoughts on paper, I was delighted to find that people read and digested them, and many even let me know their thoughts on what I had written. It was a wonderful validation of my work, and I thought that would be the end of my book writing journey. I had a "been there, done that" kind of attitude.

But my learning never ended. First, I continued to gain knowledge from all of my workshop participants and consulting clients. They have validated much of what I have suggested as good process, emanating from my lived and learned experiences. At the same time, they led me to up-to-the-minute models and new problems to explore.

Second, I had the unique opportunity to design and lead a research project focused on inter-agency collaboration with the Wellesley Institute. It was a fabulous learning experience to work with so many experienced researchers and assemble the learning about collaboration into one project report. My thanks to everyone associated with that project. I want to especially thank Pauline O'Connor, my co-manager of the IASC project, for her laser-sharp mind that helped me become more discerning of and focused on the questions I explore.

And then lastly, I learned from the writing process itself. I picked the brains of some of the best collaborative practitioners in my part of the world. Thanks to Anne Gloger, Joe Torzsok, Linda McGrath, Mark Cabaj, Jon Harstone, and Sylvia Cheuy for sharing your amazing successes and challenges with me.

My deepest appreciation is directed to Joe Torzsok and Anne Gloger who reviewed my draft manuscript. They both spent hours reading and digesting the material and provided in-depth feedback. Thank you both for having as much passion as I do for the world of inter-organizational collaboration. Our learning journeys have intersected in many ways and I thank you both for your willingness to include and support me.

I am most grateful to my editor extraordinaire Janice Dyer for helping me edit my manuscript and providing great feedback and thoughtful comments. Thanks too to my graphic designer Andrea Douglas of BEAR Design who has worked with me on many projects over the years.

Lastly, I want to thank my children and friends and family for being so supportive and helping me through the inevitable periods of procrastination that go along with the writing process.

Joan Roberts
Toronto, Canada
November, 2009

Figure 15: Logic Model Process reproduced with permission of
the Shaping Outcomes project (www.shapingoutcomes.edu), a
course in outcomes based planning and evaluation developed for
the Institute of Library and Museum Services, a federal agency,
by Indiana University Purdue University Indianapolis (see site for
acknowledgements).

Pearson Education Ltd granted permission for the use of Figure 4
Organizational Culture Web adapted from Figure 2.5 'The Cultural
Web of an Organization' from their publication 'Exploring Corporate
Strategy' by Johnson & Scholes.

ISBN no: 978-0-9865271-0-4

TABLE OF CONTENTS

CHAPTER 1 COLLABORATIVES:
A new form of organizational structure

He who would lead, let him be a bridge.—Welsh proverb

Why write this book?

In the five years since I wrote *Alliances, Coalitions and Partnerships: Building Collaborative Organizations* I have continued to teach practitioners, work with collaborative organizations, and undertake research in the area. Meanwhile, an academic literature on process has emerged, emphasizing to collaborative practitioners the need for good process to ensure successful outcomes. Amidst all the attention on process and trust building, however, there is a lack of literature on governance, including the lack of a basic primer on the how to's of collaborative governance. This is not surprising to someone who teaches this topic, as governance as a focus of concern for non-profit organizations has only emerged in the last 20 years, and within that emerging literature there is little agreement about what constitutes effective governance. (Bradshaw et al, 1998)

In the absence of agreement of what constitutes good governance in the NPO sector and a sparse literature on good governance process in collaboratives, I am venturing to fill the gap for practitioners. This book will:

- present an overall conceptual framework based on the six-step framework presented in my earlier book;

- provide references to theory and literature;

- suggest good governance practices for collaborative organizations; and

- provide a toolbox to create an appropriate governance structure for the stage of collaborative development.

This book is a response to the needs articulated in the Inter-Agency Services Collaboration (IASC) Project. It is grounded in as much evidence as currently exists on good governance practices, along with learning from my own work and interviews with other practitioners.

Process innovations often have a wide ranging—even revolutionary—impact on society. This book explores the development of a major process innovation that is taking place within our organizations, and the role governance plays in creating successful inter-organizational collaboration. This innovation is challenging the workplace to adapt to complexity, but at the same time is adding much complexity to our jobs as we adapt to technological and political change. Inter-organizational collaboration is a complex solution to complex problems. This book is meant to help build a map to help navigate the new territory and build organizational infrastructure.

As we moved toward the 21st century, a revolutionary process improvement emerged at the grassroots level of business and government service delivery: the joining together of organizations. When two or more organizations come together for shared service delivery, back office support, or to work together to change policy, they need to create a new hybrid structure to support these joint activities. The technical term for this new organization is *trans-organizational system* (TS). Common terms used to describe trans-organizational systems include alliances, coalitions, networks, partnerships, joint ventures, and consortiums[1].

TSs are functional social systems existing between single organizations and societal systems. They are able to make decisions and perform tasks on behalf of their member organizations, although members maintain their separate organizational identities and goals (Cummings, 1984).

In other words, TSs are organizations of organizations; the organizational partners retain their autonomy and legal structure, but together form a unique structure for shared decision-making and joint benefits. Over the last few years, the term collaborative has emerged to describe this organizational form, and I will use the term throughout this book.

In my first book, *Alliances, Coalitions and Partnerships: Building*

---

[1] For a formal glossary of terms, go to www.joanroberts.com for the *Inter-Agency Services Collaboration Project Report*. A glossary of terms is provided at the end of the report.

Collaborative Organizations, I presented a six-step development framework and a model of organizational effectiveness. This model included three focii: trust building, work coordination, and governance. This book provides a more in-depth look at the role of governance in developing and maintaining a collaborative organization. Governance is perceived as a board function in the NPO (non-profit organization) sector, and may be invisible to those used to a service delivery function. My key message is that although there may not be a collaborative board in place, there is still a need for governance. This book provides a step-by-step system to create a successful collaborative and governance structure.

From one collaborative practitioner to another:
I have worked in government and the NPO sector for over 35 years in Toronto, Canada. As someone who is mission-driven to create a healthier community, I have assumed many roles: community organizer, elected official, and collaborative leader and practitioner. By adapting to the needs of different levels of government and different sectors, and rolling with the ups and downs of the social economy, I have worked in health, health promotion, public safety, immigration and settlement, municipal government, and economic development. I have trained every possible type of worker in government and the NPO sector, including the military. Without a doubt, every government and NPO worker is facing increasing complexity, rigid bureaucratic systems, and unending service demands. I hope that the information in this book will help reduce the feelings of being overwhelmed reported by many practitioners, and provide a way to achieve positive change desired by all. I care deeply about people who devote their lives to help others, and hope you can find something in this book to help you on your quest for social justice and a better world.

Collaboratives are Process Innovations
Since processes are hard to patent (and harder to enforce) and cannot be sold easily in product form, they are not usually money-makers for their inventors. However, their impact is often far more widespread than most new products or services. In the case of trans-organizational systems, there is no sole inventor attributed to the innovation. The invention of processes is happening in the business world, and also by activists, politicians, non-profit leaders, and government bureaucrats. The idea came to so many at the same time largely as a result of new computer and internet technology.

Organizations are the basic structure for most of our human activity, including work, family, and recreation. A crowd has no need or purpose with which to collectively channel its energies, so it is not an organization. In contrast, a family channels its energy and knowledge to nurture the physical and emotional need of its members, and is thus an organizational or human system. The basic purpose of an organization is to transform knowledge in some way. In families, we learn continuously about our partners and children and adapt our actions to meet their needs and support their individual growth. As a result, learning and knowledge transformation take place even in families. For instance, imagine you have a child who wants to play soccer. You hear this desire, and then create a plan to enroll the child in lessons, and even schedule family vacations around tournaments. As any parent knows, a lot of work-like activity goes into raising children.

Frederick Taylor became one of the most influential process innovators of all time by inventing what sociologists call the "Division of Labour." Up until the early 19th century, workers controlled the entire production process from start to finish[2]. A single worker in a carriage-making occupation, for example, would build the entire horse carriage. Carriage-making was a fine occupation that gave the worker status, control over the work process, and many opportunities for personal expression and creativity.

However, since the process of building a carriage was as time-intensive as producing some pieces of art, Frederick Taylor decided that the process could be simplified and standardized, saving time as a result. The innovation removed the creativity, such as decorative carving, that was originally contributed by a skilled craftsman. Small business craftsmen did not appreciate this innovation, even though Taylor was a political progressive and felt he had the interests of workers at heart. He believed that by designing jobs for unskilled labour and transferring control from a skilled craftsman to a group of workers, fewer jobs turned into many and mass production turned workers into consumers. [3]

Taylor's division of the work process into smaller pieces of work transferred the responsibility for control and coordination to a supervisor instead of the individual worker. The supervisor decided how to handle technical issues and made any decisions so the workers could perform their small piece of the work process unhindered. Taylor spent his life promoting his process improvement, but never made the fortune one would think he deserved. Instead, Henry Ford turned Taylor's process improvement into the assembly

[2] Although the process called the Division of Labour is credited here to Frederick Taylor, others including Adam Smith had written about the concept as early the 18th century, and Karl Marx in the first half of the 19th century.

[3] The result of this process innovation helped catalyze development of the modern economy.

line, and used it to produce affordable cars for the middle class. Taylor's process improvement influenced everything from educational practices to child rearing, and greatly influenced the origins of modern bureaucracy. We all live with his legacy every day, but his name is unknown to most of us.

A number of other process improvements occurred in the 20th century. For example, the development of autonomous corporations from an economy of family-owned businesses facilitated the development of the modern economy with large corporations led by professional managers rather than small companies led by family members. We would not have a global economy without this process improvement. In addition, quality improvement processes, as developed by William Edwards Deming and adapted by the Japanese, led to the decline of the American car manufacturing sector. Another process improvement with wide-reaching impact was the management trend to flatten hierarchical organizations, thereby eliminating levels of management and instead using ad hoc teams or workgroups to manage organizational change and new projects. These examples show how a process innovation with little hype and no marketing campaign attached to it can be incredibly transformational.

Process innovations can help us adapt to changing conditions, and can also result from technological change. Both private and non-profit sector companies always keep an eye on the competition, and have to plan and react so they maintain or increase their share of the market. This is a process of knowledge transformation. Companies do market research to gain knowledge of what is happening in the market place, they transform it into a plan for new products or services, and then execute the plan. Organizations in government and the non-profit sector do this too, but often have more variables and knowledge inputs from multiple layers of stakeholders. They too must gather information from all their sources and then transform the information into new knowledge, new plans, and new interventions to address social and economic problems.

However, problems are now so complex that we have outgrown the capacity of our existing free standing organizations to respond. We face complex interrelated problems with inadequate financial resources, especially in the government/NPO sector, while often the solutions we need are rooted in many different systems, from the individual to family to neighbourhood to community and societal. We have had to discover new ways to bring people together so that our organizations are more than the sum of the individuals and organizations with an interest in the issue; we must also engage the target population or service users. This is challenging because front line workers and service users rarely understand the social and bureaucratic fragmentation and divisive competition over limited resources that NPOs face in the struggle to develop programming.

To adapt to complex and turbulent change and achieve the size or flexibility required to deal with this complexity, we are undertaking large-scale process innovation. By adapting the basic form of organization, we are creating a hybrid organizational form we are starting to call collaboratives.

What is collaboration?

The activity of a collaborative is collaboration. When we speak about collaboration in general, the term refers to a group of people working together to reach a common goal. Collaboration can describe a group of people working within an organization or external to an organization.

For this book, I use the term *collaboration* to refer to inter-organizational collaboration—a coming together of autonomous organizations—although there may be individual members participating on their own behalf. The terms partnership, coalition and alliance are often used to describe these joined-up organizations. These terms are used interchangeably in the NPO sector, and can range from loosely organized to more formal structures. I use the term *NPO* as a catchall for all the organizations driven by a mission to serve, as opposed to those focused on generating a profit, such as private businesses. Under the NPO banner, I include charities, sector organizations, human services, and volunteer-run organizations. As the collaborative process innovation takes root in each sector, major differences in use and approach are emerging. Although many in the private sector will identify with and can make use of this book, I am speaking to those who are serving in some capacity in the non-profit sector.

A collaborative is distinct from a purchase of services or a contractual arrangement due to the need for ongoing decision-making and a governance structure that requires regular meetings to resolve issues. If the area of focus (a marketplace, a clientele, or a target population) is constantly shifting and requires constant adaptation, then you have to decide if the additional investment of energy and capacity is worth the effort of building a collaborative. Normally a transactional arrangement between a buyer and seller does not need a collaborative structure. There may be a payoff from building ongoing relationships with suppliers and vendors, but investing in costly capacity building should be used only when a collaborative arrangement is the best solution.

In the private sector, relationships with suppliers, vendors, and customers are considered the source of innovation:

In 2007, Hewlett-Packard Company (HP) sponsored an online contest to design the skin of HP's new special-edition entertainment laptop. The company promoted the contest selectively in 13 countries via the television, Web, and mobile channels of its media partner, MTV Networks. But word spread virally, and more than 8,500 entries poured in from 112 countries in just over a month. The contest site got more than 5 million hits, prompting HP to re-forecast sales to five times its original estimate. And it was "all because we opened the doors and allowed our customers to design our products," says Mike Mendenhall, HP's chief marketing officer.[4]

As a result of this kind of private sector innovation, NPO funders are motivated to press their funded organizations to get closer to their customers through community development initiatives. The goal is to achieve this same kind of close customer relationship that might catalyze change in the NPO sector.

Figure 1 describes the types of collaboration in which government and NPOs engage.

Figure 1: Types of Government and NPO Collaboration

Comprehensive Community Initiatives (CCI)
The term *comprehensive community initiatives* (CCI) describes the full range of initiatives that take a comprehensive approach to change within communities to improve the well-being of their residents. These initiatives "indicate a commitment to change at many levels, including individual, family, institutional, and community-wide," through processes that involve collaboration and coordination within the community and between the community and the broader society (Kubisch et al., 1998).

---

[4] *Digital Darwinism* by Christopher Vollmer 5/11/09, in *Strategy+business* Booz & Company.

Inter-/Intra-Governmental Collaboration

As the complexity associated with social problems has increased for NPOs, so has it also for governments. Governments are crossing jurisdictional boundaries to combine forces and resources to tackle complex problems. Increasingly, in societies with federal systems of government where there are shared jurisdictions with states or provinces, only by cooperating and addressing the common issues can any progress can be made. In some areas, governments are creating collaborative arrangements between themselves (intra) and other crossover levels of government, such as federal and provincial (state). *Horizontal* is the term most often used to describe this governmental process innovation. Horizontal initiatives can involve multiple departments in the same government, other levels of governments, and transfer agencies that receive funding to deliver services.

Inter-Organizational Collaboration

Inter-organizational collaboration can range from a simple partnership between two agencies to create a referral protocol for shared clients, to health-promotion processes that sometimes incorporate over 100 members. Advocacy coalitions fall into this category; they are created to aggregate the political power of their member organizations to influence the government's policy-making process.

Government and other funders encourage this form of inter-organizational collaboration to foster better relationships and promote service delivery rationalization. In addition, funders occasionally assign a system planning role to an inter-organizational collaboration, which is a very exciting use of this organization form in the policy-development process.

An inter-organizational collaboration includes:
- a common agenda, vision, program, or function;

- two or more autonomous organizations who maintain their separate organizational governance systems while creating a new trans-organizational system (to manage and oversee the collaboration);

- shared investment of time, energy, resources, and risk.

All of the above may be specified in a formal agreement. Table 1 details what each form of collaborative is used for.

Table 1: Uses of Collaboratives for Social Change

WORK DONE IN COLLABORATIVE ORGS/ ORGANIZATIONAL FORM/MECHANISM	INTER-ORGANIZATION COLLABORATION (TRANS-ORGANIZATIONAL SYSTEMS)	COMPREHENSIVE COMMUNITY INITIATIVES (COMMUNITY-WIDE NETWORKS)	INTER- AND INTRA-GOVERNMENTAL COLLABORATION (INTERNAL AND INTRA GOVERNMENT NETWORKS)
Policy and advocacy	These functions often occur when a few NPOs come together to advocate for an issue. Short-term advocacy efforts might not need a formalized relationship, so effectiveness is tied to a flexible structure.	CCIs can consolidate the power of many actors and focus the advocacy efforts of individual and organizational players across a sector, neighbourhood, or community. Can be highly effective, but needs lots of coordination.	Collaboration is necessary to deal with inter-jurisdictional overlap or gaps, and to build a political constituency within and without government for new policy direction. However, when governments engage target populations in policy development, it is not collaboration unless decision-making power is shared.
Coordinated service planning and delivery—program focused	Planning phase may be informal and organic until a clear focus emerges, or can be quite shallow due to funding incentives. Wellesley Institute IASCP study found formalized collaboration was rare as shared program delivery needs formalized relationships and ongoing governance.	Planning for new services is often undertaken by a large planning group or network, but service delivery can be too focused a function for CCIs with a community-wide focus. The service delivery is usually better assigned to a one partner or smaller group of partners where implementation issues can be managed more easily.	Service system planning needs to be undertaken with transfer agency partners to ensure successful implementation. Government funders provide policy direction, incentives, and funding to encourage coordinated service delivery. In the event of jurisdictional overlap, all governments need to be at the table. To support innovation in their transfer agency sectors, governments often need to overcome their own silos first.

WORK DONE IN COLLABORATIVE ORGS/ ORGANIZATIONAL FORM/MECHANISM	INTER-ORGANIZATION COLLABORATION (TRANS-ORGANIZATIONAL SYSTEMS)	COMPREHENSIVE COMMUNITY INITIATIVES (COMMUNITY-WIDE NETWORKS)	INTER- AND INTRA-GOVERNMENTAL COLLABORATION (INTERNAL AND INTRA GOVERNMENT NETWORKS)
Back office system consolidation— shared IT or HR functions	This is the most promising area for increasing NPO operational effectiveness. Formalized relationships need shared service agreements and sector supports to broker relationships.	CCIs are focused on large-scale change initiatives and can be used to broker relationships or provide education on shared service arrangements, but they are not a good fit.	Government funders can provide policy direction incentives and funding to encourage bottom up initiatives. Shared service initiatives are often an outcome of intra-government collaboration, and many local and provincial governments participate in these arrangements.
Community strategic planning for revitalization	Implementation of a strategic plan may evolve into the need for a formal autonomous organization. This does not have to be a trans-organizational system; it can be a single entity/ NPO, but inter-organizational shared governance can be highly effective if lead organizations have the trust of the wider community.	CCIs can be very effective for this kind of large-scale change. Community economic development initiatives and neighbourhood change projects fit into this category. Organizational and political complexity increases exponentially with the number of partners.	Too far removed from grassroots to provide much leadership, but governments can partner with local initiatives and invest in the strategic priorities identified by local collaborations. Community-based collaborations do the political work of building support for new strategies and policy initiatives by astute governments.
Health promotion behaviour change campaigns	Often a few major players will collaborate to focus their resources to address a particular health issue. The time needed for the change process is often the factor that determines whether a tight formalized structure is necessary, or if an informal one is needed for a one-time project.	Broad-based coalitions focused on prevention of a particular health issue are very common in health promotion. Asset-based development approaches require a broad-based CCI mechanism. A lot of time is required to communicate and manage different needs and perspectives across a sector or community.	Can provide policy direction and funding participation as members in some cases.

What problems do collaborative practitioners face?

The biggest challenge is to build trust amongst the 30 member agencies and have to keep it, maintain, and address issues immediately before they fester.— Collaborative manager.

The key problems identified in interviews with many practitioners who support the day-to-day work of collaboration include:

- determining the elements that help build trust

- working without a plan

- lack of structure to support the work

- lack of knowledge and tools on the how to's

- unfamiliarity with what governance really entails and what governance is needed in a collaborative

- cynicism and burn out

- stress that comes with working in uncharted territory

Many collaboration practitioners are technically trained specialists who find themselves in the position of supporting a collaborative process to achieve their personal performance objectives. They are not trained in adult education or community psychology, but need to know how to move a collaborative process forward. Practitioners are often highly skilled at program delivery, but have never engaged in a governance role. More than anything else, the political nature of inter-organizational collaboration stymies the everyday work of practitioners. Although most everyone wants to see the greater good served, organizations and departments have inherent self-interest at play.

It is very difficult to build a successful collaborative when some members are there just to ensure that nothing happens to jeopardize their own agency's interests. However, this situation is unavoidable; it comes with the highly political territory of NPO service delivery and social change. To counteract this very-likely dynamic, you can build a governance structure that is transparent and provides space and time for conflict to surface and be resolved. Through the tools and guideposts provided in this book, the uncharted territory of social change solutions can be mapped, surveyed, and inhabited peacefully.

What problems do collaborative funders face?

Collaborative project funders struggle with how to manage or reduce the risk where the potential for conflict and failure is high. They need assurance that collaborative-run projects will be productive and address their prioritized social problems. Funders can be just as ideal-driven as the practitioner, and want success just as much. To them it is like betting on a horse — which project will finish and win the race? Just as a horse race gambler hedges his bets, the funder looks at ways to manage the risk of collaboratives to have them move closer to a successful outcome. This book provides funders with a model to reduce the risk of reinventing the wheel, and includes tools they can use to help ensure success.

What is governance?

Governance includes the organizational structures and processes that are power-based, that enable conflict to be resolved, and that support the organization to complete its work. In my book *Alliances, Coalitions and Partnerships: Building Collaborative Organizations*, I defined governance processes as the processes that use the power mandated to or assumed by the trans-organizational system. Power is the energy that authorizes members to build the organizational structure, engage in decision-making processes, and adopt policy; in other words, to build and operate the governance structure. The power expressed through the governance arrangements guides the organization toward undertaking its work. Without any power (energy), nothing will happen. Once the power of the members is aggregated (by coming together), the energy must be channeled into one direction by agreed-upon rules and processes so that the energy can support the desired change.

So basically, power is the energy, and the governance framework consists of the rules and mechanisms to guide the energy. If a group does not agree on a date to meet, there will be no meeting and no decision-making. This creates a situation where the power cannot be channeled and used productively. However, once there is a governance rule of meeting the third Monday of every month, this rule provides enough structure to have someone facilitate bringing the group together.

In autonomous NPOs, the governance structure is believed to be the domain of the board of directors. The board makes the larger decisions about both the NPO's direction and roles. However, in a collaborative, a steering committee usually guides the process. If a board is put in place and incorporated, the organization ceases to be a collaborative because the board of directors is now the legal decision-making body and will enter into contracts on its own behalf. With a board of directors, the collaborative organization is autonomous and no longer legally accountable to the organizations of origin, even with certain arrangements like voting rights put in place.[5] In contrast, in a collaborative, the accountability of decision-makers is not only to the collaborative organization, but also to their home organizations. One cannot be extricated from the other, as happens with a stakeholder relationship. The organizations are coupled together, but not merged into a new autonomous collaborative organization.

When a collaborative addresses governance issues, it is exploring options and making decisions about the following:

- priority setting

- type of organization structure

- roles and responsibilities

- decision-making processes (voting and conflict resolution processes)

- procedures to follow to make decisions

- oversight processes including monitoring and evaluation

- stakeholder management and community representation

- image and reputation management

- external environment relations—public and sectoral advocacy

- meeting procedures

History of NPO Governance

We have had legislation governing charities in Ontario, Canada since the mid-1800s. Whenever there was a clear social need and a desire to fill it, well-intentioned people would organize a new charitable organization to address the need. The scale of service delivery changed when the welfare state emerged post-World War II, and government set about providing needed services to its population. By the 1970s, many were questioning that orthodoxy. Large government-run public housing complexes had turned into stigmatized ghettos, and the human service system became bureaucratized

[5] In the legal documents, you can specify that founding organizations have certain privileges, such as a guaranteed seat on the new board, but legally the directors when sitting at the board table of the new organization must ethically and legally put the interest of the new organization ahead of the interests of its own organization.

and was accused of demeaning the marginalized and at-risk population. Devolution to the NPO sector was seen as a humane alternative. Devolution of public authority to other levels of government and decentralization of responsibility for service delivery to local agencies, boards, and commissions have also been important instruments in the public sector trend toward collaboration (Armstrong, 1998). At the same time, economic restructuring in the 1990s encouraged neo-conservative beliefs that forced the sector to become more competitive in the manner of the private sector. Despite attempts to curb expansion[6] and incorporate market-based dynamics, the NPO sector continues to grow, due to ever-increasing need and demand for services (the byproduct of those same market dynamics) and the determination of people who strive to overcome the obstacles and try to fill the gaps in people's lives.

The non-profit and voluntary sector is an economic force in Canada. It accounts for 6.8 percent of the nation's gross domestic product (GDP) and, when the value of volunteer work is incorporated, it contributes 8.5 percent of the GDP. If one sets aside the one percent of organizations that are hospitals, universities, and colleges, the remaining organizations contribute 4.0 percent of the nation's GDP.

Non-profit and voluntary organizations employ 12 percent of Canada's economically active population, and provide 13 percent of its non-agricultural employment. Excluding the one-third of paid employees working for hospitals, colleges, and universities, the sector still employs nine percent of the economically active population, and provides 10 percent of the non-agricultural employment. The entire non-profit and voluntary sector engages nearly as many full-time equivalent workers as all branches of manufacturing in the country.[7]

Program Delivery Models Versus Governance Structures

Those who work in NPOs often face an overwhelming urgency to make a difference. That feeling often creates a high pressure environment to deliver a program or service as soon as possible. As well, computers have sped up work processes by imposing rapid communication that leads humans to feel pressured to react quickly. Mistakes and poor thinking can happen when adequate time is not spent building organizational capacity and planning. A

---

[6] See IASCP report, *What Does Government Want?* for an exploration of government statements and objectives for collaboration in the non-profit sector in Ontario, Canada.

[7] Michael H. Hall, Cathy W. Barr, M. Easwaramoorthy, S. Wojciech Sokolowski, Lester M. Salamon. *The Canadian Nonprofit and Voluntary Sector In Comparative Perspective.* © 2005 Imagine Canada.

colleague, Dr Jane Cooke Lauder, wrote extensively about the impact of this sense of urgency, called a drive to action by collaborative members in South Africa. Leaders of collaborations in the circumstances she examined felt that spending time on anything beyond agreeing to the issue or opportunity was not valued. Action is preferred because it does not permit the membership the time or space to explore covert assumptions and divergent interests (Lauder, 2008).

Practitioners feel good making decisions regarding a new program because the program is the intervention strategy to address the social issue driving the collaborative. Making decisions also delays tough conversations. When developing a program, the following types of decisions need to be made:

- What type of services will we provide?

- Where will the program be delivered?

- When will it be available?

- To whom will it be made available?

- How many staff will we need? What skills do they need?

- How much will it all cost?

- What is the unique differentiator/value proposition for this program above others?[8]

To most people in the human service sector, program planning is fun and satisfying work. We can visualize the new program helping people, and this can be a powerful motivator to keep going despite adversity. In an NPO, most of these decisions are often made by staff or a program committee. This is fine in single organizations, but if a collaborative is formed by program delivery staff, there may be a tendency to focus on program development and not address organizational and governance capacity issues. The desire to avoid addressing organizational self-interest at the collaborative table can be an unconscious norm with any organizational member, including management, board, or staff. Gaining an understanding of organizational governance will help staff, especially those in program delivery, to understand the broader organizational issues that plague inter-organizational collaboration.

Why is governance important for collaboratives?

---

[8] Reviewers of the pre-publication manuscript emphasized that often in their experience, little thought is given to the value proposition.

Governance is the work of providing direction to the organization while resolving conflicting needs, ensuring there are resources and that they are managed appropriately. A traditional NPO creates a board of directors to fulfill the governance role. In contrast, a collaborative may never create an autonomous board of directors, but it still needs to address and fulfill the governance functions undertaken traditionally by a board. Regardless, the decision-making body providing oversight must:

- represent the interests of member organizations and the broader community;

- make sound business decisions;

- manage the finances;

- minimize risk to the collaborative and the member organizations;

- understand the collaborative's legal roles and responsibilities;

- understand their individual responsibilities;

- know the difference between governance and management; and

- manage any professional or administrative staff.

All of these functions must be undertaken while working as a team and building trust so that the partnership will work. Saying that, it is important to note that governance structures gain in importance and detail as the work progresses. A simple governance structure like a Terms of Reference is enough to get a group up and running. But as more tasks and resources develop, a more elaborate governance arrangement must evolve.

At the beginning of a collaborative, the work is to figure out what the problem set is and how to address it by bringing together all the knowledge and other resources available. Having a clear decision-making process is the most important tool for resolving the different perspectives around the collaborative's table. This decision-making process then allows the collaborative members to co-create the rest of the governance structure.

NPOs work in a field of high conflict characterized by competitive funding arrangements and turf or power issues between members, within changing economic conditions. In the environmental sector, for example, collaboration is clearly used as a mechanism for conflict resolution, and collaboration researchers often use the term collaboration interchangeably with conflict resolution. For this sector, the end result of a collaborative process is usually a policy framework that is supported by multiple stakeholders.

In contrast, in health and other sectors, this conflict resolution function of collaboration is not as clear. Nonetheless, it should be understood that a collaborative is a new complex organizational structure whose primary function is to enter into unexplored territory that it intends to inhabit and develop in some way. Using the metaphor of land use planning, one needs to determine several things: Is this unclaimed space a rural or urban area? Is it territory worth exploring and developing to meet human needs, or should it be left as forest or agricultural land? In other words, how much development is appropriate?

It's a different journey into new territory each time. For some early North American explorers, it was the search for the mystery and riches of the east. For others, it was the search for the Northwest Passage. For astronauts, it's the mystery of outer space. For social entrepreneurs and change agents, it's the mystery of solving the unsolvable social issues of our time; the desire to move large systems, like health and social services systems, government bureaucracy, and communities, and to make them more responsive to the needs of citizens.

The modern world was built upon the metaphor that humans and society operate like a machine. All the parts of the machine were knowable, controllable, and predictable. Just as machines can be maintained and oiled, fixed, and parts replaced, this metaphor underpins the way we approach human systems. Using engineering and efficiency practices, we have pressured humans to conform to the needs of the machine, to have set hours of work, to coordinate all parts of the assembly line to work in tandem to ensure that all parts of the machine work interdependently. Our schools have supported the mass production economy by churning out workers who conform to the needs of the factory. In my day, we got a prize at the end of the year if we did not miss a day of school. The result was that this child would make an exemplary factory worker.

Although this was the way of the world when I went to school, factories are now far and few between in North America. Our society and economy are now considered post-modern, and are highly complex and constantly evolving. New technologies arrive daily, spurring on new industries and jobs unheard of even two years ago. Our communities are fragmented; people no longer congregate around old institutions like church and family, but instead gravitate toward lifestyle enclaves or affiliate to communities of interest. This changing disparate society is difficult to harness and move in any particular direction. As a result, it's difficult to organize people to meet social challenges. Political parties use sophisticated polling and behavioural techniques to attract voters, but this methodology is very costly and does not focus people on solving social challenges, except for fundraising purposes. As a result, unsolvable social challenges get a lot of political rhetoric that sounds like something is being done, but in reality nothing much is accomplished. Collaboratives are a grassroots response to meet these social challenges. By aggregating the political power of a number of organizations and attempting collective action, there is often enough of a critical mass to begin large scale change.

In determining the boundaries of a problem, in deciding who sits at the table, and in choosing what strategies are used, collaborative members are making decisions in a new space outside of their traditional organization's boundaries. Who makes all these decisions is determined by who has the power to decide. One example to consider is a coalition to end homelessness. Causes of homelessness are the driving issues of the coalition. If coalition members are primarily housing providers or developers, then that perspective is going to drive the definition of the problem. In contrast, if its members are primarily mental health service providers, a mental health program model will most likely be the dominant paradigm. However, if the coalition consists of members with multiple perspectives, each perspective will get incorporated into the problem definition and strategy and they will find themselves in a new space for problem solving.

If you subscribe to this notion that collaboration is a mechanism of conflict resolution in an emerging complex territory, you might then see the value of collaboration as a mechanism to aggregate political will and power. If one can get the actors in a system to make similar decisions, then that behaviour reduces the complexity of the multitude of choices and produces change in an emerging system.

Role of collaboratives in the broader governance structure—government
While the focus of this book is on the governance structure of inter-organizational collaboration, collaboratives are increasingly seen as a force in the broader governance structure of our communities—government. For the UK Labour government in 1997, collaboration was seen as an ideological counterpoint to free market philosophy:

Inter-agency collaboration in the public sector has been viewed as a self-evident virtue in complex societies for several decades, yet has remained conceptually elusive and perennially difficult to achieve. Paradoxically, these problems have not diminished governmental enthusiasm for it—indeed, if anything, the pursuit of inter-agency collaboration has become hotter. This is particularly so of the United Kingdom, where the 1997 Labour government has been ideologically anxious to jettison the emphasis of the previous administration upon markets and competition. Collaboration—or 'partnership', as the Government prefers to describe it—seemed the ideal alternative. (Hudson et al, 1999).

Governments (often of the opposite ideological ilk than those mentioned above) also see the limits of solitary organizations when addressing clients presenting with multiple problems; they state they are striving for coordinated collaborative responses. Often this is exposed as a veiled attempt to download health and social service responsibilities to more junior levels of government and to the NPO sector.

Along with community engagement, network and collaborative governance are new areas that are being explored within the public policy field. The proponents of these terms are looking at ways to engage the population in the activity of governing and making policy.

> We appear to be entering an era of 'governance without government'; a policy making environment in which coordinating power and control is shared between the major 'collective actors', requiring more sophisticated organizing mechanisms to make it possible. The underlying dynamic and trajectory of change in governance systems suggests a move away from the 'hierarchy paradigm' towards the 'network paradigm'. This shift in governance introduces a higher degree of decision-making complexity. In particular, the decoupling of previously vertically integrated corporate decision-making hierarchies, in both the private and public sectors, presents intractable coordinating and control problems. Nevertheless, these developments seem to demand innovative ways of thinking about and practicing the 'new arts of network governance'.
> (*Voluntary Sector Forum* by the New Economy Development Group, 2005)

As sweet as this sounds to change agents, keep in mind that any new proposed policy always has to be adopted by decision-makers, therefore I am keeping it outside the scope of this book. There are some overlaps, and policy-makers and their members will often see community-based collaboratives as legitimate stakeholders in policy-making. However, due to legislation, it is virtually impossible for decision-makers to relinquish their decision-making role or governance role and truly collaborate; they always decide. And as this book is training you to govern, albeit an organization, the skill set taught in this book is not necessarily the one needed in the policy-making arena of collaborative governance.

When collaboratives collaborate across horizontal boundaries, they are entering unexplored territory with ambiguous boundaries and unclear rules of engagement. It is therefore critical that members establish a governance system with the capacity to be resilient — that is, to respond quickly to new conditions, events, opportunities, and problems, and to adapt and change its procedures and relationships as needed. Just as Christopher Columbus quickly adapted when he realized the new world he found wasn't China by convincing his financial backers there were many riches in the new land anyway, social change explorers need to be open to the riches collaboration can bring without knowing exactly what form the riches will take.

CHAPTER 2:
Why does governance in collaboratives need to be addressed?

There are no short cuts to any place worth going.—Beverly Sills

This chapter introduces the topic of governance and its role in building collaborative capacity. Barriers that impede effective inter-organizational collaboration will be identified, as well as findings of the IASCP (Inter-Agency Services Collaboration Project) report. In addition, the chapter examines governance themes from practice and research, including issues like community ownership, conflict resolution, formalizing structural arrangements, and the impact of collaborative governance on your home organization. The chapter concludes with an introduction to the six-step development model that will be explored in detail in chapters 4 to 10.

Although my personal preference is to emphasize the need for people processes and those activities that build trust in a collaborative, the importance of trust building and good process is very evident. In 2007, I had the privilege to lead a comprehensive research project on inter-organizational collaboration in the local non-profit sector. The resulting reports are listed in the bibliography. To begin the project, we undertook a literature review looking for evidence of successful outcomes of collaboratively-run projects. However, most of the academic literature up to that date (2007) was focused on the processes that bring about successful partnership.

In looking at the research, a gap emerged in terms of identification of effective governance processes. In my consulting work and the IASCP study, we found that most collaboratives in Toronto had not yet reached a stage where they had to develop an organizational infrastructure to implement project plans. Many projects considered themselves to be collaboratively-run, but their focus was at the communication stage where they shared information, or at the cooperative stage where they developed shared referral protocols.

Figure 2: Continuum of Types of Inter-Agency Collaboration, by Intensity

	LESS INTENSE			MORE INTENSE
INDEPENDANCE	COMMUNICATION	COOPERATION	COLLABORATION	INTEGRATION
	INTER-AGENCY INFORMATION SHARING	SHARED POLICIES OR PROTOCOLS FOR DEALING WITH CLIENTS	SHARING RESOURCES STAFF, DECISION-MAKING	INTEGRATED PROGRAMS, PLANNING, FUNDING

Adapted from Vanderwoerd, J. (1996). Service Provider Involvement in the Onward-Willow-BBBF Project: 1990-1993. Better Beginnings, Better Futures Research Coordination Unit: Queens University

Through the IASCP initiative, we found that practitioners were not yet easily moving into the stage of collaboration. Some of the learning from that project revealed that NPO staff may lack the higher-level skills and personal capacity needed to embark on complex partnership building, which requires individual agencies to negotiate across organizational boundaries (Graham, 2007; Roche & Roberts, 2007). As well, the two process-oriented studies in the project identified the need to establish an appropriate governance structure, since a collaborative structure requires mechanisms for transparency, power sharing, conflict resolution, and other inclusive strategies (Roche & Roberts, 2007; Roberts, 2007).

Despite the lack of track record, participants in the key informant study felt that community-based agencies want to collaborate more often and more intensively (Figure 2) wherever doing so will leverage more resources to respond to the complex needs that agencies face (Graham, 2007).

What governance barriers impede effective inter-organizational collaboration?

As inter-organizational collaboratives succeed and mature, practitioners and funders are increasingly identifying governance challenges as impediments to success. Alexander, Comfort, and Weiner (1999) conducted research involving over 25 community health collaboratives. They identified the following top five governance issues:

- Clarifying partner organizational roles, responsibilities, and relationships

- Designing mechanisms for ensuring community accountability

- Increasing community involvement and ownership in the partnership

- Creating and sustaining collaboration

- Growing and developing partnerships

Shortell et al. (2000) identified six factors in achieving effective, sustainable collaborations. The first three factors ("managing size and diversity, managing and channeling conflict, and 'handing off the baton'") deal primarily with political issues associated with maintaining a strong partnership or coalition. Thus, the successful partnerships had incorporated a political element into their models, and the successful partnerships that could leverage support for more funding (Boutillier, et al, 2007, p. 47).

In interviews and documents, collaborative practitioners identified these governance issues:

- *Everyone has a stake in the collaborative but no one owns it.*

- *Competition and turf issues prevent the building of trust. There is an ongoing need for conflict resolution. Collaborative members need to commit to resolving the issues and determine how they will go about it.*

- *When is the timing right to build the infrastructure? You don't want to scare people off and you need a lot of flexibility at the beginning.*

- *When Executive Directors send juniors to meetings, we get saddled with permission seekers rather than decision makers.*

- *One respondent from a group that undertakes a number of collaborative initiatives reports that half of their projects have implementation issues. These are low returns on the investment of time and energy.*

- *As time goes along, many collaboratives report their largest and ongoing governance issue is how to how to access funding resources without incorporating and losing the collaborative structure and shared member control. To have a trustee or incorporate, that is the question.*

- *A particular problem in the non-profit sector comes from the huge turnover of staff. So many staff are underpaid or work on short-term contracts that they come and go throughout the life of a collaborative. This creates an ongoing need to constantly build trust, communication, commitment, and an organizational memory that can include newcomers quickly and efficiently.*

Governance Themes from Practice and Research

Ownership
The first governance theme is how the division of power occurs in the interface between "community" ownership of the collaborative and ownership by the agency members. Almost every society today has political institutional arrangements that clearly articulate responsibilities and accountabilities of government and the non-profit sector. Community ownership of government is manifested by the political arrangement of representative democracy. Community ownership of NPOs is obtained through appointed or elected community based boards of directors. However, collaboratives usually forgo incorporation and an autonomous board of directors because they are counter-intuitive to the shared decision-making that a collaborative arrangement permits.

Without a board, a collaborative is only accountable to its members. Although the member organizations all have boards, the accountability to the community through a non-elected board of directors may become very tenuous. One author calls it a legitimation crisis:

- Where are the lines of accountability drawn?

- How does the community as owner get played out in the collaborative institutional arrangement?

- Does the community get a voice?

- Does the community need to have a voice?

Conflict Resolution
The second governance theme is conflict resolution. Both the literature and practitioners report the overwhelming need for conflict resolution. The nature of the organizational form is that you often have members competing against each other in the quest for financial resources or target markets. The task becomes

to figure how the collaborative can develop processes to work out cross-organizational allegiances and turf issues.

But conflict emerges within the individual as well. To whom are the individuals most accountable—their home organization or the collaborative? What happens when there is conflict between the interests of the two? How do they get resolved? Does the home organization have policies and reporting procedures to guide individual representatives?

> Each governing board member of a community-based partnership typically wears two hats—one as a policy-maker and leader of the partnership and another as a representative of his or her organization. (Alexander, Comfort, & Weiner, 1991)

There are also conflicts and dilemmas inherent in the complex issues that collaboratives address. To reiterate, the focus of the collaborative's entire field or domain is characterized by conflict. If there was no conflict, the problems would have already been solved. In addition, if the collaborative successfully navigates the early challenges and gets to the point of service delivery, it then faces the tension between partnership growth and development. How do you handle/balance growth, especially when growth of the partnership puts the collaboration in the role of competitor to the member agencies? Resolving conflict is never-ending when organizations collaborate.

Formalizing Structural Arrangements

Some research has now established the need for formal governance arrangements. In my own practice and research, the most effective collaboratives are those that construct governance arrangements as soon as the collaborative begins to meet. Processes to give members a voice in decision-making and meeting management are needed immediately. But as practitioners often say, an overemphasis on building organizational capacity will scare people off early in the process. The art of practice in the early stages is to construct just enough structure to have people around the table making decisions and building enough trust to move through the planning phase.

Determining the role of community, collaborative agreements, policy frameworks, conflict resolution processes, resource investments, organizational structure, and evaluation are all governance issues that need to be resolved in formal agreements and documents.

Impact on Governance at Home

Engaging in inter-organizational collaboration challenges the governance of the home organization in many ways. First, the community ownership and oversight function remains with the agency board of directors. My local health system coordinating body is encouraging implementing NPOs to undertake program integration across organizational boundaries, and calling it voluntary collaboration. Concerned that the reporting and oversight activity of agency boards is so far removed from the day-to-day activities of the integrated programs, they are exhorting the agencies to report more frequently so the bureaucrats can identify a clear line of accountability. But crossing organizational boundaries adds levels of complexity that challenge the internal controls of autonomous organizations.

Collaboration challenges the authority structure of an organization. As an individual, it can be confusing to experience the freedom of shared decision-making that takes place in a collaborative and then return to an agency with a command and control culture. From a managerial perspective, you need to be clear on what your staff are empowered to do. And then when they do it, you need to live with the consequences.

Employees may fear working in collaboratively-run projects not only because of the unclear reporting, accountability, and reward structure, but also because they see collaboration as a threat to their status in their organization. Certainly much of the work in collaborative projects goes unrecognized and may not even be mentioned in job descriptions or work plans. Funders often require client contact statistics. If a staff person's time is spent in meetings building trust and exploring complex problems, when evaluation time rolls around the member's time may not be able to be measured and recognized as easily as others. In addition, once a collaborative is up and running, there may still be inadequate and uncoordinated data collection and lack of outcome information. Staff members may fear the impact on their performance records and careers and may be reluctant to get involved in something so ambiguous.

In the case of professionally trained staff, the nature of a collaborative process often invites service users to integrate their unique perspective. Empowering that constituency requires power sharing on the part of the professionally paid and trained. This leveling of the playing field is often a messy and hurtful process to the participants, as the service users can resent the power position of the professional over their lives, feel alienated by the jargon and expertise of the professional, and use the opportunity to challenge the professional's status and knowledge. Expecting staff to engage in collaboration can pose great managerial and governance challenges, and can severely test the culture of the member agency.

Ten Critical Success Factors

In addition to the themes identified above, governance is interwoven into all the factors needed to ensure successful collaboration. The following ten critical success factors for collaboration were gleaned from the recommendations from each of the IASCP reports and the report from a roundtable discussion of the human service delivery system. All of the success factors are related to governance.

#1 MOTIVATION TO COLLABORATE

Motivation to collaborate is critical to the success of collaboration. The desire to address gaps in service delivery and resource enlargement are NPOs' principal motivations to collaborate. Forced or incentive-driven partnerships designed by funders may have unclear motivations that are not in the interest of participants. For example:

• Is the organizing issue compelling enough to maintain interest and commitment?

• Are there clear benefits to undertake collaboration?

• Is there a clear value proposition?

• Is the problem complex and not able to be addressed by a sole organization?

#2 ENVIRONMENT IS READY

For a collaborative to be successful, the following environmental conditions must be met:
• Conditions are favourable in the external environment.

• Funding is available.

• Convener and convening leadership is seen as legitimate and acceptable.

• Collaboration members have developed collaboration skills and built some inter-organizational trust from previous efforts.

3 POWER ISSUES ARE ADDRESSED HEAD ON

Collaboratives are consumed with power and turf issues!
• Boundary negotiation is constant – boundaries around the problem, the boundary around the system, and interpersonal boundaries.

• Ambiguity reigns – attribution of power must be worked through in the decision-making process and governance structures.

#4 GET THE RIGHT PEOPLE

Ensure the people and organizations involved in the collaborative:

• have an interest in the problem;

• have resources (not only financial) that can address the problem;

• have the skills to co-create boundaries and negotiate the creation of a new structure;

• are organizational representatives that can act; and

• will do the work between meetings.

#5 TERMINOLOGY

Agreement about the terms used to describe collaborative arrangements and the target issues must be a widespread goal. Professional jargon impedes trust building across sectors and with lay people. Organizations should move toward adopting the same definitions. Until these terms have been widely agreed upon, an emerging collaboration needs to develop shared definitions of collaboration before beginning their conversation.

6 FIND COMMON GROUND

Development of a unique purpose and common vision is critical. Begin the process with self-interest, but to continue you need to transcend differences to find common ground. Along with an agreed-to common vision, the project needs clear measureable goals and objectives that can be linked to outcomes.

#7 SUFFICIENCY OF FINANCIAL AND OTHER RESOURCES

Financial resources are necessary for the extra time to build inter-organizational relationships in a collaborative process. Insufficient staffing prohibits the organizing of meetings and the work to implement intervention strategies. Smaller agencies, although motivated to collaborate to access needed resources, often have little extra financial capacity to invest. However, they bring skills and expertise, information, and connections to target populations.

#8 LEADERSHIP AND PARTICIPATION

Everyone in a multi-organizational collaborative experiences some form of culture shock and culture clash. Culture is a belief system; organizations and sectors all have many covert beliefs that only come to the surface when

(The six-step model is adapted from Thomas G. Cummings, Transorganizational Development, in Research in Organizational Behaviour, (1984), JAI Press, Vol 6, pages 367–422.)

you work with people from outside your group. Collaboratives need lateral leadership processes and role modelling to bridge the diverse cultures, perform boundary-spanning functions, and reveal and challenge assumptions that limit thinking and action. Change management tools from organizational development and adult education can help work through difference.

Good collaborative processes are necessary to improve outcomes. Participative processes are needed to develop a vision and for governance, especially decision-making, trust building, and the coordination work amongst multiple partners. These processes can facilitate the egalitarian leadership and commitment needed among disparate and autonomous partners to co-create a new mission and collaborative organization.

Inter-organizational collaboration requires a range of skills, often high-level. This complex skill-set includes all the skills required to run programs and organizations, and the ability to deal with a high level of conflict and change leadership competencies. Programs and training need to be made widely available to enable the people who will lead successful collaboration. In addition, poor relationship building among organizations leads to a failure in collaborative efforts. Relationships are built over time, so time and energy must be allocated for this.

9 ROLE AND STRUCTURAL CLARITY

Members need to understand their roles, rights, and responsibilities, and how to carry out their responsibilities. A flexible governance framework needs to be developed to ensure participation, clear roles, and the policies needed to support the work. Implementation strategies require a flexible organizational structure and multi-talented generalists as staff. Once developed, it is wise to formalize arrangements in a partnership agreement.

10 COMMUNICATION

Coordination of communication among partners and partnership activities and the preparation of materials makes it possible for multiple independent people and organizations to work together. When there are only monthly meetings, ongoing communication can be supplemented with newsletters, email broadcasts, Intranets, and other technologies. Maintaining a group memory is critical if there is member turnover.

The IASCP research substantiated the logic of the six-step model. We will next use the six-step framework to explore building the governance framework for a collaborative.

Figure 3: The Six-Step Development Model

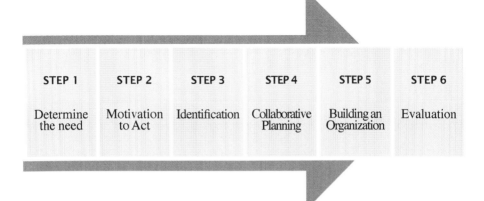

Over time, practitioners and researchers have developed practical tools and frameworks to help promote the success of multi-organizational processes. As pioneers exploring new territory, we observed the nature of the terrain over time, and we are now aware of the hills and valleys of building relationships across organizational boundaries. The six-step framework is a road map substantiated by research and developed through the practical experience of building programs and social change campaigns delivered through collaboration.

STEP 1 – DETERMINE THE NEED FOR A COLLABORATIVE AND EXPLORE THE PROBLEM SET
The first stage begins with the organizing issue. What kind of issues prompt people to look to other organizations for help? Steps 1 and 2 are strategic thinking and planning questions for conveners and members to consider prior to joining or starting a collaborative initiative.

STEP 2 – MOTIVATION TO ACT
Moving outside of your organization's walls can be the beginning of a leadership journey. The roles and skills required to work in a collaborative are different than those required in a traditional government or NPO workplace. Examining your own motivation is the foundation for building the driving force to collaborate.

STEP 3 – IDENTIFICATION—WHO SHOULD BELONG?
This is the member identification and recruitment stage where political dynamics emerge and need to be considered.

STEP 4 – COLLABORATIVE PLANNING—SHOULD A COLLABORATIVE ORGANIZATION BE CREATED, AND IF SO, WHAT IS ITS WORK?

The common vision and action strategy are developed at this stage. To move diverse organizations and people toward collective action, a participative and inclusive planning process is necessary to build trust and find common ground.

STEP 5 – BUILDING AN ORGANIZATION—HOW DO WE ORGANIZE THE VISION AND ACTION INTO STRUCTURE, LEADERSHIP, COMMUNICATION, POLICIES, AND PROCEDURES?

At this step, the group develops the organizational infrastructure needed to implement the common vision and plan. Internal organizational processes are needed to streamline the ongoing work and decision-making.

STEP 6 – EVALUATION—REFLECTING ON AND CONTINUING THE PARTNERSHIP

The final step is the evaluation phase, which can complete the entire process or begin anew in whatever form the members decide. Evaluation of both process and outcomes is needed.

By moving through the six-step model, you will make governance decisions in a systemic way. In this way, you will develop just enough structure for the process to move forward, but not enough to bog down participants in building capacity before they have agreed to their intervention strategy.

Some of the governance decisions that you need to make in developing a successful collaborative include:

- What is the problem or set of problems you are trying to address?

- What language and jargon will you use?

- What is your mandate? What is your purpose? What kind of business are you in?

- Where does your authority to act come from?

- When making decisions, who do you need to participate in decision-making?

- What decision-making processes will you use (voting and conflict resolution processes)? How do you make decisions? Consensus or majority rule?

- What kinds of decisions will you be making?

- What are the roles and responsibilities of the chair, members, treasurer, vice-chair?

- What type of organizational structure will you use? Hierarchical command and control versus democratic or laissez faire?

- What procedures will you follow to make decisions (policies)? Who takes the leadership to develop a policy? How will you make policy?

- What oversight processes will you use, including monitoring and evaluation?

- What is the role of the stakeholder (e.g., funders and regulators and community, including other NPOs and the users/consumers/taxpayers)?

- Who is responsible for image and reputation management (more than just branding in the corporate sense)?

- What external environment relations will you need (e.g. public and sectoral advocacy)?

- What meeting procedures will you follow (e.g., how to have effective meetings)?

Not all of these questions may need to be answered in your particular case. There is no single best way to govern a collaborative. Human service organizations and governments are extremely complex organizations to begin with. Adding new layers of organizational capacity external to the existing structure just adds to the complications of already difficult work.

Each of the governance themes identified in this chapter will be explored throughout the remainder of this book. I will not be presenting a simple linear model, as the governance framework and structures need to be constructed in accordance with the unique needs of the collaborative, taking into account its unique mandate, membership composition, and its programs, activities, and funding. Instead of a step-by-step prescription, I will look at the developmental process and present tools and frameworks to help you, the practitioner, pick and choose the appropriate next step to gain success and work with the complexity that exists in your particular situation.

CHAPTER 3:
Getting your agency or department ready to partner!

If you do not change direction, you may end up where you're heading.
—Lao Tzu

Chapter 3 focuses on the role the home organization plays in creating successful external collaborations. Many benefits can accrue to a non-profit organization through inter-organizational collaboration, and the chapter begins with a short review of these benefits. The chapter then explores a common scenario that takes place in collaboratives all over the world, which illustrates the leadership and policy vacuum in which organizational representatives involved in collaborations frequently find themselves. I also provide an organizational assessment to help you determine how ready your agency or department is to collaborate. The assessment results are analyzed to help you build a foundation within your home organization for successful external collaboration, and prepare you and or your staff to participate in a collaborative.

The most frequently cited benefits to collaboratives as cited by practitioners include the following:

• Generates the ability to accomplish more with the same resources by joining up organizational resources and forming a larger pool to address issues.

• Accesses a diversity of perspectives and energy to address a complex issue. Can bring together many specialties or professions at the table without cost (i.e., instead of consultants).

- Helps to protect programming, or increase its size in time of fiscal restraints.

- Helps access alternative sources of funding.

- Fosters innovation, generates excitement, stimulates new energy by reducing feelings of organizational isolation and powerlessness.

- Leads to new perspectives on new ideas/what's going on as a result of new relationships. The collaborative becomes a network that helps with others issues.

- Helps agency become involved in broader community building. Opens up dialogue between organizations that are competitors.

- Permits management to bypass some original structures by working outside of the organization's boundaries (e.g., union/contractual rules).

- Generates career opportunities for individual staff and allows them to acquire new and different skills.

- Enables lateral inter-organizational communication.

- Enables the collaborative community to better react to crisis because of the collaborative structure.

- Becomes the mechanism to overcome resistance to change or narrow views amongst the members of the delivery system, over time.

And finally, collaboration amongst service delivery organizations may also reduce duplication and increase efficiency in the overall use of resources — but the practitioner/academic jury is still out on that. Every so often, collaboration and merger as the solution to the unstated problem of "there are too many NPOs" becomes the flavour of the month for funders. They believe it wholeheartedly, even when there is no research to support the belief and an emerging body of knowledge identifies the resource-heavy investment collaboration requires before the payoff of system awareness and change can occur.

In Ansari and Phillip's (2001) study of the costs and benefits to collaborative participants, interviewees identified the following costs:

- The partnership activities don't always reach the intended beneficiaries.

- The time spent on the partnership keeps individuals from doing their work.

- Sometimes the member organizations don't get enough recognition for their contribution.

- Implementation is fraught with difficulties.

- Individual skills and time are not well-used.

Everyday Scenario:

Jama is a health promoter just hired to work in diabetes prevention at a community health centre. One of her ongoing tasks is to attend meetings of the local Diabetes Prevention Coalition. Her manager has introduced her to the coordinator of the coalition, who happens to work for the local public health department, and told her the details of the next meeting. The manager also provides her with the minutes that the previous staff member filed neatly in a folder.

Excited to meet new people, Jama goes to the next meeting. She is introduced to all nine members of the coalition and takes her place at the table. She sits quietly and tries to take in all the discussion. The coalition seems to be at a critical juncture, and members are discussing their overall strategy to reduce diabetes rates in the community. Most of the options people are discussing focus on choosing behavioural interventions to reduce diabetes, such as urging people to eat better and exercise more. But Jama believes that social determinants of health, like income and poverty, are more important to work on than individual behavioural change. She believes if people could afford better food, they would buy it. She feels an advocacy strategy advocating a food supplement for people on social assistance is a better option for the coalition's work. Should she speak up?

She does not know whether her employer would approve of her opinion. Does the community health centre support a social determinants approach? Nobody said anything to her. How about suggesting advocacy? That could be a real no no. Jama decides it is too risky to say anything. After all, she thinks, these folks have been meeting for over a year. Surely her supervisor knows what they are doing.

She decides she will send the minutes to her supervisor when she gets them.

You might be thinking: there goes another opportunity! Have you ever experienced anything like this? Have you gone to a meeting and had no idea of your organization's position on a hot topic? I certainly have.

Is Jama at fault for not speaking up? I don't think so. Ideally, she will go right back to her office and corner her supervisor and debrief the scenario. Her supervisor will have a policy or position statement that states what approach the agency favours and give it to her. If not, the topic presents the opportunity to make one.

This is just one example. Collaborative members need to know all kinds of organization parameters to fulfill their representative function at a collaborative table, such as knowing if they can spend money, how much of their time to contribute, as well as the organizational interests in the focus area. The staff person needs to briefed and guided on all of these issues before ever going to a meeting.

In my experience, very few NPOs are prepared to effectively or strategically collaborate and engage in partnership. Engagement in collaboratives/ partnerships needs to be a conscious decision for an organization so that the organization's representatives are empowered to act on behalf of the organization in the decisions of the collaborative. If you begin developing a collaborative from the premise that each participant has a self-interest in the outcome of the process, then the home organizations need to be clear of what exactly is that self-interest.

While most NPO collaboratives are focused on delivering better services or improving organizational effectiveness, some academics are seeing NPO/ government member collaboratives as new systems of governance for the political system. So, while the focus of this book is on developing governance systems for the collaborative, others developing the field in political science are talking about creating a new form of governance for entire societies or communities. When you create a collaborative across a domain (like one involving all the mental health agencies in a community), the result is a new social system. That social system can govern the behaviour (to some extent) of those member organizations. Many people become aware that they are pioneering much more than they were initially aware of. They may be self-governing systems in the same way professional colleges are, or they may take different forms. All in all, something new emerges.

> If you're really in one of these new systems of governance, your board has less strategic room to move and make choices. You're dancing to the tune of a piper (or even more likely, multiple pipers!) beyond your organization's boundaries. In other words, the governance of your work has moved beyond your organization's boundaries (and your organization no longer has the kind of sovereignty that it once had). (Renz, 2006)

For better or worse, when agencies engage in collaboration they find themselves engaged in a shared power dynamic where they have little to no power over the other partners. The energy to move forward comes from learning about each other and working together to develop a common vision or agenda. To make decisions, the collaborative needs to build a governance structure that all the members can live with and work within. But often governance and management systems are not very strong in NPOs, and the cultural bias toward program delivery can lead to forgetting the need to build infrastructure.

Before getting involved in building external governance and management mechanisms, an agency needs to look at itself. Can it operate in this new territory where individual powerlessness and ambiguity reign, that requires a different kind of infrastructure and accountability, as well as different skill sets than traditional management or program management require? Before saying yes to an invitation, it is prudent to determine whether your organization has the capacity to effectively engage in partnership.

You may wish to complete the following organizational assessment to determine whether your organization is ready to embark in a collaborative process.

Organizational Assessment: How ready is your agency or department to partner?

Please answer yes or no by putting a Y or an N in the box beside each statement. When complete, add up the yes responses and find the interpretation of your answer.

MISSION AND STRATEGY:
☐ We have a clear mission and purpose.

☐ We engage in strategic planning every 2–3 years.

☐ The board and staff participate in the planning process and understand the rational for our strategic direction.

☐ We enter into collaborative initiatives when they fit with our mission and strategic plan.

FINANCIAL*:
We have solid financial systems, including:

☐ Financial policies and procedures

☐ Bookkeeping records

☐ Staff devoted to maintaining financial systems

☐ Staff with the skills and procedures who can handle the tracking of monies involved in collaborative initiatives

*This is good practice for any NPO, but if the agency is uninvolved in contributing funds or flowing through funding to the collaborative, then this advice is unnecessary.

GOVERNANCE:

☐ We have a clear organization chart with reporting lines.

☐ We have an organizational policy framework, including financial human resources and communication policies, to help guide staff on decision-making in collaborative processes.

☐ The board has a written policy on partnership.

ORGANIZATIONAL CAPACITY:

☐ We have a track record of engaging in productive, successful partnerships.

☐ We have an inventory of partnerships and processes in which our staff participate.

☐ We have clear reporting mechanisms and procedures for staff to report on partnership activities to managers and the board.

☐ Our internal evaluation processes cover collaborative projects.

KNOWLEDGE/EXPERTISE:

☐ Our members, clients, and community need us to address the organizing issue.

☐ We are gathering information from members, clients, and the community about their needs, wants, and preferences with respect to the organizing issue.

☐ There is likelihood of organizational compatibility with other member organizations in areas of common interest and complementary capacity.

☐ The organizing issue is a complex problem that we cannot address by ourselves.

HUMAN RESOURCES

☐ We invest in our organization's human resources so they can assume new challenges and work outside our organizational boundaries.

☐ The staff who will participate in collaboratives have the skills to manage a complex change process.

☐ There are rewards or incentives in our organizational systems (i.e., performance appraisals) that will motivate staff to engage fully with collaborative initiatives.

ORGANIZATIONAL CULTURE

☐ We have a flexible supportive culture that trusts staff to be offsite and make decisions within set parameters.

☐ Our organizational culture supports learning and personal development.

☐ Staff and management believe there are benefits from participating in collaborative ventures.

☐ Our organizational culture supports risk taking and experimentation.

Checklist Score

NUMBER OF YESES:

0–13 The whole idea of the organization engaging in collaborative processes should be rigorously questioned. If collaboration is strongly needed or desired, the organization should engage in an internal change process to build the internal capacity.

14–19 The organization is moving in the right direction, but the infrastructure to support collaboration needs more attention if the organization is going to be successful at collaboration.

20–25 The organization is ready enough to embark on successful collaboration. The challenge is to maintain its awareness and member role in collaborative projects and link the work of collaborative processes into the strategic direction of the organization.

Why are these organizational capacities important to have before embarking in collaboration?

Your organization's mission and current strategy:
Self-interest in an NPO is rooted in the organization's mission or purpose. Empire building is often a disparaging term to describe NPOs and their leaders who are on a course of growth and expansion. But social change organizations can be just as entrepreneurial (and need to be to make social change) as for-profits. It's just that the drive to expand is motivated by the desire to serve more clients rather than sell more product. NPOs compete for funding and resources, and many NPOs use partnerships as a strategy to secure more resources for growth. In one of the IASC projects, we found partnership development was often a survival strategy for small organizations

or communities that were struggling for resources and credibility with funders.

Effective collaboration can only happen when the participants know why they are there and express what their agency needs out of participating. When an agency wants a piece of the funding but does not say it and comes away without it, as in the example above, resentment will foster feelings of disempowerment and accusations of power mongering by those that get what they need. At the beginning, organizations often don't really know what they might get, so they play along until they can determine if there is something in it for them. Others aren't even aware of all the processes their staff participate in. But time is money. If your staff members are engaged in external processes where they spend time, your organization needs to get something out of it to make the time spent worthwhile, and to ensure that it is helping your mission and is aligned with your organizational strategy. If your organization does not have an up-to-date strategy, how can you determine whether the collaborative process will support it?

For example, a number of community-based service providers are meeting to determine how they can enhance their service delivery to the physically challenged community. After a number of meetings, they identify the need for a mobile library that can provide service to homebound clientele, and decide they will work together to make it happen. Although one agency provides services to the physically challenged and sees the project as a great addition to the service mix, it has a strategic direction to expand the skill sets of its personal attendants. It decides that working on the library is not a good use of its time when they desperately need to upgrade the training provided to its staff. Its staff opts out of the collaboration, wishes everyone well, and spends their extra time developing a training needs assessment.

If your organization does not have a strategic plan, then decisions to opt in or out of opportunities to collaborate will be made according to whim rather than strategy. It is very important that you get your act together before you can develop a new act.

Financial:
If participants in a collaborative cannot develop a budget or monitor expenditures in their home organization, why expect that they will be able to do so in a collaborative? Yet this happens all the time. Program staff represent their agencies at the collaborative. When the collaborative is entrusted with money, someone with management skills needs to ensure it is managed properly. Home organizations need to have policies in place to

ensure the proper management of funds in the collaborative in which they participate. Unless one agency assumes a trustee function, financial policies and systems need to be in place to govern the spending of monies. If your agency's name is on the letterhead or on a proposal submitted to a funder, you have a fiduciary responsibility. That responsibility needs to be spelled out in your organizational policy, and your financial management staff need to be involved so that your liability is minimized, even if the money does not come to your bank account.

Governance:

As discussed earlier, governance in a collaborative is a function and not necessarily a role, unlike a board of directors in an NPO. Collaboratives rarely develop boards of directors because the home organizations have their own boards, which they want to keep. By creating a new board, the organization would be autonomous and not as tightly accountable to member organizations. So, the function of governance has to be assumed by the collaborative members. However, if your organization's representatives have no board experience or knowledge, how is the governance function going to be implemented? If your organization has not trained its board members and executive director in governance, who has the skill set to transfer this knowledge to the staff? Do you have a partnership policy that delineates what kind of governance decisions your staff can safely participate in without impinging on the legal authority of your own board?

These questions and others will come up eventually. If your organization is comfortable with policy making, you can develop policy to address these issues so you need not reinvent the wheel every time they arise. Other issues to consider include:

- What do you expect your staff to report about to their supervisors about the activities of the collaborative?

- What issues are important enough for the board to decide?

- If you don't have a policy-making board, how will your staff know how to assume the governance function in their work?

- How should you address these issues?

Organizational Capacity:

In the IASC project, we discovered that many small agencies pursue inter-agency collaborations as a survival strategy to meet the criteria of funding programs. Although the intent of these funding programs is sometimes to build capacity and transfer knowledge between small and large agencies, smaller agencies often lack the ability to participate in the same way as more endowed agencies. Smaller agencies may not have any resources to contribute, aside from attending meetings and providing access to a target population. If the larger partners use their capacity to build the collaborative, manage the incoming funding, and manage staff, smaller agencies may begin to suspect there is a great imbalance to the partnership.

If you work in a smaller agency, I urge you to think hard before engaging in a collaborative with larger agencies. Consider the following questions before making a decision:

- Do you have staff capable of co-managing the complex funding and staff arrangements involved in collaborations?

- If you don't get any of the funding, what will you get out of the project?

- Can you invest the time needed to build a collaborative mechanism, or are you thinking only of the funding?

- Is your time better spent building your home organization?

Are you aware of all the partnerships your agency is involved in? I have heard of mid-sized agencies involved in upwards of 70 collaborations. Boards and executive directors need to explore whether they are meeting expectations, or if they are just window dressing for political purposes. The bottom line: If collaborations are not moving the agency forward in meeting its mission, they should be discontinued.

Knowledge/Expertise:
Collaboration occurs when there is an issue that can't be solved by one organization. Usually one organization decides to convene a number of others who have different perspectives and resources to help address the issue. You need to consider the critical issues that matter to your organization because there are so many issues that need to be addressed. Which ones are your organization's priorities? You also need to decide why these issues are your organization's priorities.

Other issues to consider when deciding whether or not to participate in a collaborative include:

• What does your agency bring to the problem solving process?

• What specialized knowledge or expertise can you share to help diminish the complexity of the problem?

• Is it crucial that your agency participate, or can another agency from your sector fulfill the role?

You should not participate in a collaborative unless you are absolutely sure that you will bring some clarity, expertise, and specialized knowledge to the problem definition and solving process. One caveat to that is the case of an advocacy coalition, where all the power holders privy to an issue need to participate to aggregate the political power necessary to push or back policy makers.

Human Resources:
NPOs are hard-pressed to invest in human resources. The cultural onus to invest every spare penny in programming makes it difficult for boards and management to invest in its staff. The impact of this system-wide behaviour is coming home to roost: As baby boomers retire, the following generations are not keen to take on mission-focused jobs with low wages and little training or professional development.

The skills required for collaboration are higher level skills than those required for day-to-day program and management work. Not only do staff members need to be knowledge resources on the complex problem that is probably related to their professional training, they also need to have management and governance competencies and the skills to manage a complex change process.

In the private sector, a new job classification has been developed called *strategic alliance* manager. Each collaboration is assigned to a strategic alliance manager who manages the interface with the partners in terms of governance and management. This manager also manages the interface with the home organization and its internal systems (e.g, finance department). New professional programs have also been developed to train these professionals. Because they are generalists who are spanning organizational boundaries, they are seen as staff members who have a direct path to the CEO office.

Whereas these positions are considered high status positions in the private sector, in contrast the responsibility for collaborations is often downloaded to as many untrained people as possible in the NPO sector. Unfortunately, funders and NPO leadership fail to quantify the impact of investing staff time in large-scale change initiatives for which staff are not prepared or trained.

Organizational Culture:
Organizational culture is a vague term, but it is quite powerful in the life of an organization and cannot be easily changed. Organizational culture is the unseen music that underpins the day-to-day life of an organization. It emerges from the shared assumptions and behaviours of its members as the organization interacts with its environment. If a government or funder requires stringent reports, the culture adapts to that external stimuli. A department can also develop a culture due to professional training and allegiances, mandates, and roles (e.g., health promotion versus enforcement).

Figure 4: Organizational Culture Web

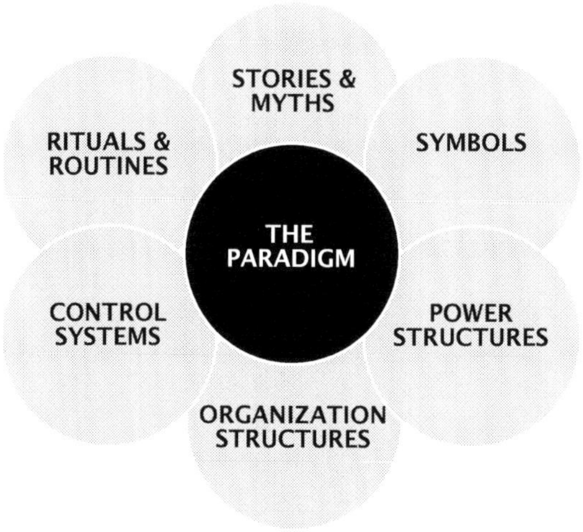

The cultural web graphic is adapted from Gerry Johnson and Kevan Scholes in Exploring Corporate Strategy, 1992, Prentice Hall.

As Figure 4 illustrates, organizational culture is determined by many things. Employees tell stories and myths that get passed along. Corporate symbols are chosen with certain values and messages in mind. Over time, power and organizational structures evolve. Depending on the nature of your organization, control systems like funders or the board of directors monitor your processes and people. You may find that certain procedures work, so you develop routines that allow you to do the same thing over and over. All of these aspects of organizational life contribute to the unique stew of organizational culture. NPOs may have unique organizational cultures that are different than the private sector in that they are often female-dominated and mission-driven, but they are still run as hierarchical organizations. The collectives that used to exist in the women's services sector have almost all turned into hierarchies. Banks and funders refuse to tolerate the time it takes to work through democratic processes and the ambiguity when no one is in charge and accountable.

So, for almost all of your work life, you reside in hierarchical autocratic structures with the vestiges of command and control management that create an organizational culture. Then you get the opportunity to develop and participate in a power sharing democratic collaborative, but the rules and power systems are much different. The culture is different as well. The question that no one asks is: How does the staff person who represents your organization bridge the two very different cultures?

Consider these issues:
- Is the staff person used to a culture that welcomes participation in decision making, or are staff told what to do?

- What happens to staff if they make a mistake?

- Do staff members know better than to take a risk without getting permission first? If so, can you predict how they will behave in a collaborative?

More likely than not, your staff will make few contributions to the collaborative due to lack of experience. If you do not want your staff to react this way, there are things you can do to loosen up your own organization's culture:

- Give staff members some practice with making decisions.

- Engage staff in organizational issues.

- Reward curiosity rather than submissive behaviour.

- Create a learning organization at home before attempting to build one with others.

Agency Policy on Partnerships:
I will discuss policy development for the collaborative in greater detail later on in the book. However, you can capture your thoughts and answers to the questions identified above and record them in your organization's policies.

The following tool will help you develop an organizational policy for participating in collaboratives.

General statement on what the organization needs from its collaborations.

Some suggestions:

• To advance the mission/vision of the organization

• To leverage resources, tap new opportunities, and generate new revenues for the organization's mission

• To enhance the organization's public image and reputation

• To improve services to clients

• To uphold certain values

What can you offer?

Specify in a general way what you have to offer to a potential collaborative. Some suggestions:

• Access to funding or a catchment area

• Access to a special population

• Extensive experience in the service business

• Capacity builder with emerging organizations

What criteria will you use to decide whether or not to participate?

If your organization does not have criteria for participation in a collaborative in place, you need to develop them. What would satisfy you that the process has promise and potential? The term *due diligence* describes the process of ascertaining whether you have looked at an organization's legal and financial structure to decide whether to invest or do business together. What kind of due diligence do you need to do with potential partners and in what situations? The exchange of monies always provokes questions like these, but even when there may be no money on the table, your organization invests in the collaborative by spending staff time. Time needs to be looked at as an investment.

Look back at your organization's previous partnering efforts, and especially the failures. What contributed to the failures? What can you ask to be done differently? Consider intangibles like:

• staff being empowered to make decisions;

• a commitment to attend meetings;

- honest participation;

- a conflict resolution process; and

- a signed agreement.

Make sure that staff members who are participating in collaboratives know these things so they can be communicated to the collaborative members at the beginning of the process.

What decision-making power do participating staff have?

This is the most critical area in which to empower staff to fully participate in collaboratives. If the work of a collaborative is to host a process to use the knowledge resources of its members to scope out a complex problem and then develop a strategy to change it, then decision-making is the most important work function after the learning function. Effective collaborative meetings share information; its members engage in learning and then decide what to do with the problem and what action to take. Therefore, decision-making is the raison d'etre for meetings. Prepare your staff beforehand so they can do the work that is supposed to happen in meetings. Effective collaborative governance is dependent on effective organizational governance within the member organizations, meaning your organization has to determine what decisions your staff can make or the governance house of cards tumbles down. Consider the following questions:

- What decisions are you comfortable with delegating to staff participating in a collaborative?

- Are staff members empowered to design new programs, apply for funding, engage in strategic planning?

- How do you want requests for money to be handled?

- Can you identify an internal approval process for non-delegated decisions?

- Who do staff go to when they are unsure of their authority?

Joint management/partnership agreements: What do you need from the collaborative?

Collaborative agreements themselves will be discussed in chapter 9. For your organizational policy, you need to determine what you want to see covered in any joint management agreements. Think ahead about how you can cover the liability risks for your organization. In the event of public events, specify how much insurance you want to see in place. Money issues are critical, and staff members need guidance on what questions to ask at the collaborative table. Be sure to specify how you want funding to be managed.

The thorniest issues are human resources issues. When hiring consultants, many collaboratives find themselves in trouble with government labour boards. Collaborative staff may take a job without being fully aware they are being retained as a consultant as opposed to a staff person, and remain unclear about who they are working for. Collaborative staff members often end up working with one agency's staff and begin to feel like a staff person rather than a self-employed consultant. Labour boards often agree with them, and hold all the member organizations accountable. Be sure to be clear with any collaborative staff and be clear with your agency staff to prevent misunderstandings.

Other HR issues that can emerge include circumventing collective bargaining agreements by attempting to keep collaborative staff outside the bargaining unit of a unionized workplace. Again, when working across organizational boundaries, staff members are often the victims of lack of clarity. For example, if a lead agency becomes responsible for managing a collaborative's staff, a lack of clarity around performance management can result. Who has the right to direct staff? Do they report to a manager at a lead agency, for instance, or to the membership of the collaborative? All of these issues need to be thought through and processes agreed upon in the legal agreements between any trustee and the collaborative.

One HR-related issue that cannot be managed with governance tools is organizational culture. Organizational culture is the unspoken rules and beliefs that the employees of an organization hold about the way things are done. In the absence of a collaborative organizational culture, staff attached to an agency will often be assimilated into the lead agency's culture without questioning whether the collaborative will want something else. This unquestioning cultural assimilation is particularly sensitive in cross-sectoral collaboratives, because it permits the culture of the lead agency and its sector to dominate when staff make unspoken assumptions and decisions.

A sample organizational policy on inter-organizational collaboration can be found in Appendix A.

Preparing staff to participate in a collaborative:
Not all staff want to leave the office and manage the ambiguity and steep learning curve resulting from participation in a collaborative venture. Others leap at the chance. For those interested in participating in a collaborative, the following tips may be helpful:

• Select staff with a higher level of interpersonal skills who are comfortable with ambiguity.

• Ensure staff members have a good knowledge base of the agency's activities, programs, and clientele. Remind them that they are knowledge sources for the collaborative.

• Begin an orientation to the collaborative or the proposed project with your organization's policy on collaborative participation. It will be your primary tool to help clarify roles and expectations and parameters for decision-making.

• Explain the benefits of participation to the agency and how participation enhances the agency's mission and strategic goals.

• Discuss the benefits to the staff members. The literature is quite clear that staff gain many benefits from participating in collaboratives. Not only does it broaden their skills and networks, it opens up career opportunities.

Before you go out and build organizational capacity external to your home organization, it is vital that you build internal capacity that will support you and your staff to face the different types of challenges that emerge through inter-organizational collaboration. Your home organization has to have good systems in place to manage day-to-day work and governance. There will be new pressures on the organization that you will have to adapt existing systems to meet, such as:

• organizational pressures that come with interacting with other organizational cultures and building a new organizational culture in the collaborative; and

• radically different skill sets needed by staff as they work external to their home organizations.

CHAPTER 4:
Collaborative Organization Structures

The universe is full of magical things, patiently waiting for our wits to grow sharper
—Eden Phillpotts

This chapter explores the structure of the collaborative organization. Collaborative members co-create the structure through a series of decisions taken throughout the process. The structure illustrates key governance principles, including power authority and accountability. It is the result of many decisions taken, not always consciously. This chapter examines the multiple factors that contribute to the choice of organizational structure, and presents the three organizational genotypes that represent the basic choices for the structure of a collaborative.

Remember: Governance is a function—this book's central message. In the NPO sector, we are used to thinking of governance as a role. But people traditionally in staff roles are now performing governance functions in community partnerships. Developing governance awareness is the consistent message; to do this, you need to create an organization structure with the governance function front and centre. This chapter addresses how to create a collaborative organizational structure without a separate governance body like a board of directors.

Governance Structure Evolves Over Time
You need to create an organizational structure right away to support the unique nature of the membership and the strategy or intervention. As soon as you form

a group and decision-making becomes a shared responsibility, you can begin to build a simple structure. When more than one person is involved, a group forms; we usually call this informal group a committee. The committee is the simplest organization structure. With one group—the committee—all the members make all of the decisions.

However, as the process becomes more complex, new components get added to the structure to accommodate staffing, more voices, and more work. In seeking to collaborate, no-one wants to build a traditional NPO structure. Instead, they look for ways to a build enough structure to support the work, yet minimize the investment of time and resources.

Governance structures somewhat reflect the work process. Your intervention strategy might require a number of task groups or committees supporting and overseeing the various projects of the collaborative. All these task groups should have terms of reference that spell out who they go to for final approval, or if they don't need any approvals. You can have as many as you like, keeping in mind that you need someone to support the work of each committee in terms of scheduling and minute taking.

Accountability: Where Is The Locus Of Power?

The structure determines who will provide oversight control and seek accountability over the work groups. There are three basic choices: no-one controls any of the outputs of the task groups; all the collaborative members form a body to provide oversight to all the working groups; or all the members agree that certain members will have the power to oversee all or some task group outputs but not others. No one course of action is better than the other—it depends on the nature of the work and the needs of your members.

Walsh et al, (2006) identified a popular governance structure in shared services collaboratives. They reported that the governance model included an overall steering committee made up of senior-level stakeholders who have a vested interest in the activities to be consolidated into the shared services operation. That group had a strategic role focusing not on the operational detail, but on the key business problems to be solved and ensuring progress. Implementation of the program was entrusted to an implementation team, a small group of individuals who work full-time and are accountable for the initiative. Lastly, they established project teams representing cross-functional groups drawn from experts in particular areas and who have line responsibility for particular activities.

Governance functions involve power, control, and accountability. Structures have to reflect how the power is assigned, who approves or makes decisions, and who needs to know what.

This evolution in governance makes sense from an organizational theory perspective. A leading perspective from organizational theory asserts that an effective organization's design will align with and reflect the key characteristics of its operating environment. Thus, if the organization's operating environment (including the kinds of problems it must address) is increasingly dynamic, fluid, and complex (with many different facets to its problems), then the appropriate organizational response will be a design that is dynamic, fluid, and complex. (Renz, 2006)

Factors that influence the design of a governance structure

1. Staffing
If there is no staff, then the steering body (may be called a steering committee, but is not a legal board of directors) has to operate as a working board, assuming both governing and staffing functions without any legal status. The collaborative members have to carry a heavy load at the beginning. The coordination work involved in supporting the meetings and ensuring the following meeting happens can take at least 15 hours per week. If there is no staff, collaborative members themselves have to devote the time to ensure that meetings happen. If there are sub-committee meetings, add on another 10 hours for minute-writing and meeting coordination for every sub-committee. Even with some staff support, their time may be taken up with planning meetings.

One staff person will be able to support the governance function of a steering body, but may not have much time to implement intervention strategies such as proposal writing and staffing a project team. Members of the steering body have to pitch in until enough staff come on board to let go of the operational work. Partnerships definitely work better with staff than without. Staffing allows for more follow-through and community outreach (Chrislip, 2001).

2. Government Mandate
Conflict resolution and building political will for change is usually the collaborative's primary function. You may find that the collaborative needs to accommodate to the dictates of a government funder or regulator. Who gets to make decisions and what kinds of decisions will determine the collaborative organization structure.

Many people find themselves involved in processes that look like collaboratives, but they are really government consultation processes. If this is the case, be aware that you are involved in a process that may be of value, but the power to make decisions will rest with government representatives who may or may not be involved in the process. As well, representatives appointed to the steering body may be direct government appointees aligned with the party in power—in effect, political actors without holding political office. You will find this kind of dynamic on bodies like regional health authorities, which are often used as a buffer for governments to make unpopular decisions and who do not assign enough power or resources to the decision-making body.

If the entity that looks like a collaborative is not the decision-making body and the resources are government staff, be warned that it is not a trans-organizational system, but rather it is a consultation process. There is nothing wrong with a consultation process. Governments need widespread consultation; sometimes it can take years before a new program or policy is even developed. Although they may be organized along an inter-organizational collaborative model, these bodies do not have the authority to share power or decision-making with citizens or NPO organizations. They are better included under the terms of collaborative or network governance as a tool to broaden the policy-making process.

3. Geographic Proximity

The geographic proximity of members influences the way the collaborative is designed. For example:

- Can the collaborative hold face-to-face meetings?

- Can technology be used to bring the steering body together to make decisions?

- Are members time pressured and not willing to participate in phone or online meetings?

As in any collaborative, all decisions do not need to be made by all members. Certain types of decisions can be prioritized and assigned to sub-committees or an executive body. If you do not have many face-to-face meetings, you need to determine which key decisions will be made by whom and what decisions need to be made in face-to-face gatherings or shorter technology-supported meetings (teleconference or web based).

4. Motivation

Recent research, including the IASC project, shows that if the collaborative is forced in some way, it is likely to result in failure. Forced or incented partnerships, encouraged by funders in particular, are unlikely to build relationships based on mutual need and respect. In the NPO sector, partner agencies will only come together to obtain the financial resources and invest only what is needed to obtain the funding.

In early 2009, the Lodestar Foundation announced the winners for its $250,000 Non-Profit Collaboration Prize. A primary goal of The Lodestar Foundation is to encourage collaboration among non-profits, highlighting that the ailing economy and fundraising anxiety should lead to collaborations and mergers as a strategy for non-profits. Four of the eight winners were mergers between non-profit organizations. Funders like to soft peddle their objective of reducing the number of non-profits through mergers by using the term collaboration. If you are involved in a merger, be forewarned that the autonomous nature of two or more stand-alone non-profits will be integrated into one entity. From two or more boards of directors, you will have only one board of directors that will perform the governance function.[9]

There is nothing wrong with mergers, and I also believe there are inefficiencies in service delivery systems that could be rectified through organizational consolidation. However, government funders in particular are trying to get NPOs on the merger bandwagon, and this can damage client services. For example, I received an email from a former student who reported that the government had forced a so-called collaboration on three service agencies. The three agencies' catchment areas were north, west, and south of a major city, serving an area of over 500 square kilometres. To go from one part to another could take up to four hours. Once the organizations had integrated, they applied for their regular funding allocations. However, they were told that since they were now one organization, they could apply for only one pot of money for their clients, whereas they had three in the past. Their clients would have to go to one of the former locations to get the service they used to get closer to home. The funders did not see the problem of having marginalized clients drive four hours for service. After all, service delivery was now efficient! These organizations had merged without being aware of the ramifications on their clients. One-time shots of money like what the Lodestar Foundation provides may reduce the pain of staff layoffs, but reduced client service is not an acceptable end goal for most of us.

[9] (http://www.thecollaborationprize.org/Media/Releases/Finalists-for-$250,000-Nonprofit-Collaboration-Pri.aspx)

5. Community Involvement and Ownership

Just as NPO board members have a governance role to represent the broader interest of community, so does a collaborative decision-making steering body. The voice of the broader public interest may need to be a lot louder in a collaborative if it is involved in comprehensive community initiatives (CCI). It is not as important if the collaborative is a small one designed to provide back office support to a group of NPOs.

CCIs often build the membership of community members into the collaborative steering body. Reasons for doing so may include the need for community knowledge that agencies do not have, the need for community buy-in or commitment to the collaborative intervention, or the need for large system change which involves community. Other strategic reasons for having community or individual members include the following:

- Structures that reflect the broader community are more credible than those that do not (Chrislip, 2001; Roche & Roberts, 2007).

- Advocacy coalitions that put front and centre the voice of the service users are always more effective than those that contain only agencies.

The collaborative then has to determine whether the community provides input, how much, and in which manner, or whether the community shares ownership of the process. If it is ownership, then community representatives must sit on the primary decision-making and governance body. If you want the community to be more involved in agenda setting and prioritizing, then you can seek the voice of the broader community using periodic consultations or planning forums. This intention to consult can be codified in a policy, or you can show the community as a membership base in an organization chart.

6. Power Relations

Governance is all about power. Most of the power associated with the governance function is assigned through terms of reference and partnership agreements with respect to decision-making (voting or consensus), rights, roles, and responsibilities. If the organization structure includes an executive decision-making body, then they will have a lot of power and responsibility assigned to them. In some cases, that may be desirable to save time and money.

If members are not conscious of who has power and there is no clear documentation of power relationships, then assumptions are made that may determine the structure of the collaborative. This actually is the most common form of trans-organizational system governance structure—an invisible one that exists in the assumptions held by collaborative members. Often the most common assumption is that one or a small group of members are making all the decisions and doing all the work. It is important to put those assumptions out there and agree to an organizational and governance structure that is clear to all members and stakeholders.

The complaint I hear the most is that some members are more powerful than others in the collaborative. I respond by asking, how do decisions get made? The reply is that they all get one vote and make all the decisions together. So then I ask, how does one agency get more power? The reply is that because some members have more resources, they get listened to and seem to have more influence with members. In this case, though the formal power is equalized in a document, members bring all kinds of informal power sources to the table. These too need to be made explicit through conversation to empower members who may not feel as entitled or privileged. I spend more time talking about sources of power in Chapter 12.

There is one situation in which one member clearly has more power than the others: when a member becomes the trustee or organizational sponsor. Although they may have only one vote or voice in decision-making, they must ensure the collaborative abides by the terms of funding agreements, and their board will be held accountable for the outputs of the collaborative. They do hold more power, but also have the corresponding responsibilities to counterbalance their power. Having a trustee as a member of the collaborative is one of the most problematic issues facing collaborative governance arrangements. But acquiring a trustee/ sponsor is one of the most common measures taken to access funding and save the collaborative from having to incorporate and develop a traditional board of directors (thereby eliminating the direct accountability to member organizations).

As mentioned earlier, the Tides Canada Initiatives (TCI)[10] acts as the fiscal sponsor for emerging collaboratives. This may be an alternative to the situation of the trustee becoming the first among equals *(Primus inter pares)*, where the trustee organization is technically equal, but is looked upon as the group's unofficial or hidden leader. Many established non-profits will act as a trustee as part of their mandate of community development for emerging non-profits, collaborative or not.

The important thing to remember is that the collaborative itself has the ability to negotiate the allocation of power, influence, and responsibility. These arrangements can change as the organization grows and the context changes.

[0] For more information go to http://tidescanada.org/focus/strengthening-charities-non-profits/

It is wise to hold explicit discussions of the power of the various members and stakeholders and how to balance, share, and distribute this power. In this way, you can keep abreast of the hidden assumptions that can lead to hurt feelings and non-participation.

7. Availability of Process Guides

If members are only used to working in hierarchical organizations, they may not have the skills to work in a participative and inclusionary manner. An inclusive process needs someone or a group to guide the process, create inclusionary processes, and ensure inclusionary and participative principles are followed. In the NPO sector, these folks are called capacity builders or adult educators. In the private sector, they are better known as organizational development consultants or facilitators. This is critically important because the academic literature is absolutely clear that without good process, the tough challenge of working across organizational boundaries and creating a democratic or self-organizing structure and culture will not be met. It is better to go with a hierarchical structure where power is concentrated in the hands of a few.

8. Organizational Values

If there is not a lot of energy for, time for, or interest in participating in the collaborative, participants may be quite willing to assign decision-making to a chairperson or a small steering committee or a staff person. This assignment of power and decision-making is much more efficient than trying to bring members from a number of organizations together to make low level decisions. On the other hand, if there is little history of working together or a history of mistrust amongst organizational members, working through what might be considered easier decisions can build the capacity and trust to take on more onerous or risky decisions.

People bring their values system to the table but rarely articulate their positions and interests in discussions based on their value system. Those who hold democratic values assume that the organizational structure will be a democratic one. Others who are used to only working in hierarchical organizations will assume the structure will be like what they are used to. Value clashes erupt in discussions about shared leadership or power versus efficiency and traditional assumptions about organizational structure.

Research indicates that a shared leadership model within the governance structure helps spread the responsibility for energizing the partnership (Chrislip, 2001; Roche & Roberts, 2007). However, if the value of efficiency dominates the discussions, there will be conflict about spending a lot of time making shared decisions about building the organizational infrastructure. Although process experts agree that spending the time upfront to reach agreement and clarity about goals and objectives results in efficient implementation, many people feel that any time spent on process is time wasted. With this in mind, temper your arguments and pick your fights strategically.

9. Member Selection

Do you want or need a membership base? This refers to organizations or individuals outside your core group of members who are involved in the work. Certainly for advocacy coalitions, a membership base enhances the credibility of the group. More members, both core and otherwise, tells decision makers that these "members" are voters who are staunchly behind the proposals you are advocating for. Sometimes health promotion collaboratives decide they need many members to foster widespread change at the community level. The problem becomes, what do you do with all these people who are supposedly members of your collaborative? Do you expect them all to come to meetings? Can they participate in some way, or do you just keep them in the loop and mobilize them for public or media events?

In the event of a membership base outside of the core organizational members, the key governance issue is how the collaborative is accountable to the members (organizational) or broader community. With a traditional NPO, you can create a membership base (sometimes the people on the board of directors are the only members) and fulfill your accountability to those members by reporting to the members at an Annual General Meeting. In this case, those members have the right to elect the decision-makers, the directors who sit on the board. This is why most collaboratives do not go this far. The founding organizations choose a collaborative to ensure their control over the activities of the collaborative, and they do not want to relinquish power to others, for good reasons.

For collaboratives involved in community revitalization, members are sometimes chosen through a snowball process (described in Chapter 8). In this kind of work, a community membership base is critical to ensure the success of the revitalization strategy, and involving as many people as possible is part of the strategy. But again, you need to figure out a role for these members. Some health promotion coalitions keep the membership in the email communication loop, and that works. The East Scarborough Storefront (Roche & Roberts, 2007) has a wide membership base. They hold regular "community speaks" forums that empower their community members to identify the issues that they want the Storefront to help address.

Keep in mind that building-in diverse and inclusive participation in partnership governance requires a disciplined approach to identifying potential members and a strong recruitment effort to ensure participation (Chrislip, 2004). Collaboratives need to be strategic and use a cost benefit analysis to determine whether the benefits of a community membership outweigh the cost of keeping them informed and engaged. You also need to consider the professional needs of the members. Some members may be quite happy with the assignment of control and oversight to other members in an executive body, but others may need to protect their organization's or profession's reputation in whatever products or messages emanate from the collaborative. For instance, many health promotion collaboratives include both mainstream and alternative health providers. In this case, mainstream health providers may need to have certain control over the messaging to comply with regulations and professional standards. They may want to ensure that they can approve any health-related messages before release. The governance structure needs to be designed with this in mind.

10. Member Skills

When designing and deciding on the organizational structure, collaboratives need to take into account the capacity of members and staff to manage the partnership. This will be discussed further in the chapter on leadership, but research agrees that inter-organizational collaboration requires higher level skills in addition to all the skills it takes to run a traditional NPO organization and its programs. If collaborative partners lack the capacity to run effective organizations and programs, perhaps because they are start-ups themselves, then it is unlikely that they will have the capacity to manage the demands and likelihood of conflict that comes with inter-organization territory.

Most NPO staff come to their work with technical training and may not have opportunities to build the interpersonal and managerial skills that they need for collaboration. Chrislip's (2004) article makes the point that collaborative staff members need the skills and capacities to support the leadership role of the governing members. He suggests that their role as process guides for the partnership and for the community may be more important than their content knowledge.

11. Accountability and Transparency

These are two buzz words for the 21st century. We hear them spoken every day by politicians and talking heads. But what do they mean for the collaborative that is performing a governance function? Well, they basically mean that the organizational and governance structure can be navigated and understood easily by an outsider. If the local newspaper wanted to know how things worked, they would ask these questions:

- Who gets to be a member?

- What kinds of decisions does the collaborative make?

- Who makes the decisions?

- When do decisions get made? Can the public come to watch?

- What kind of work does the collaborative do?

- Who does the day-to-day work and when?

- Is there staff? If so, who do they report to?

- How do the home organizations feed into decision-making and get brought into the loop?

- How does the collaborative fulfill its obligation to report to the community?

If you can answer these questions, and the answers are in writing and are reflected in your organization chart, then you can probably rest easy that you are running an accountable and transparent organization. If not, then work through the processes in this book until you have a clear and transparent structure that satisfies your membership.

The Governance Model Includes the Organization Model
As you may recall, all organizations are systems and have elements in common. All systems have a purpose for being, include people who are working together to support their common purpose, have a boundary with inputs and outputs of some sort, and collectively transform their collective knowledge to support their common purpose.

When we think of an organizational system, many of us think of an organization chart. When many organizations speak of organizational change, they consider solely the activity of changing the boxes around on an organization chart. This process of moving around boxes is better termed *organizational restructuring*. When we build an organization chart for the first time, this is more aptly called *organizational structuring*. To figure out what is best for your situation, you might shop around for organizational models.

Organizational models include:

- Resources required–Is your program fully funded or does it require user fees or a social enterprise element?

- Roles of management and staff–Do they do program work or do they just manage staff? Who reports to whom?

- Organization unit–Do you deliver more than one program with separate management for each program?

- Location–Where does the work take place? At the home office or a satellite office?

- Business item–What type of product or service is delivered?

Organization charts usually look like Figure 5, with someone at the top—either the chief executive officer or the board of directors—and all the people reporting to him/her below.

Figure 5: Sample Organization Chart

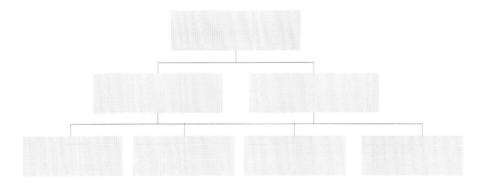

Every organization or trans-organizational system has to create an organizational model represented by an organizational chart once they are in the implementation phase or Step 5. The model evolves from all the elements at play in your context, but is focused on the service delivery component of your intervention strategy. When you include the governance functions, like strategic planning and representing the community, and practices like policy-making, then you are building the governance model.

Role of Committees in Organizational and Governance Models
Committees do the work and make decisions, but are never the final approval body. To do the work, you can have an infinite number of committees that feed

into either governance or operational management decision-making. These bodies, whether they are named workgroups or sub-committees, do the work and bring back the plans to the central decision-makers. How many you have or how many hoops they need to go through is infinitesimal, though common sense says the fewer the better.

Forms of Organizational Genotype

As stated earlier, there are three basic organizational genotypes. Kurt Lewin, founder of social psychology in the early half of the 20th century, identified them as (1) authoritarian, (2) democratic, and (3) laissez-faire. Each genotype explicitly addresses power by identifying how power is exercised through controlling employee decision-making and coordination; this is the key difference between authoritarian and democratic organizations. Laissez-faire is the organizational descriptor for an organization that does not define its power structure and lets decision-making happen in a covert manner.

The key issue you need to consider in choosing your organizational genotype is how many of the partners do you want involved in the approval and decision-making process. If time is always short, you might choose to have a hierarchical structure and empower the people at the top, whether staff or chairperson, to make certain decisions. For instance, you can have the person at the top make all the staffing decisions and on-going management decisions, but leave matters of strategic direction and money for the entire membership. Or, you can empower an executive body to share in the appropriated power. You should prescribe decision-making parameters to the persons assigned with decision-making authority in a policy, but the boundaries and reporting structure are illustrated in the organizational and governance structure.

Note that not making any conscious decisions about decision-making leaves you with a laissez-faire structure, which is desirable in only a few situations. We will explore this topic later.

The key issues to consider in each organizational genotype include the following:

- Who makes decisions?

- Who does staff report to?

- How does information flow?

Each organizational genotype must also address a possible situation unique to collaboratives:

- Is there a community base? If so, this must be reflected by a very large box at the bottom of the organizational chart.

- Is there a trustee? If so, this would be reflected by a small box at the top of the organizational chart.

1. Hierarchical Genotype: Control is vested at the top

WHO MAKES DECISIONS?
In the hierarchical model, an executive committee usually makes the decisions. This may be composed of the collaborative chairperson and manager, sponsor, or trustee, and can include member representatives.

WHO DOES STAFF REPORT TO?
In the hierarchical model, staff most likely report to the partnership manager and/ or the executive decision-making body.

HOW DOES INFORMATION FLOW?
Everything flows into the centre, into the executive body. The output from this committee might be only the decisions made, and identification of any decisions that need to be ratified by the broader membership. The dominant information flow is from the bottom-up, and decision-making is top-down, as shown in Figure 6.

Figure 6: Flow of Information in a Hierarchical Genotype

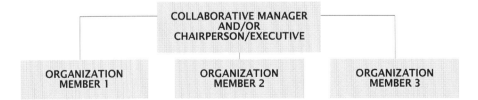

2. Democratic Genotype: Control is vested at the centre

WHO MAKES DECISIONS?
Decisions can be made by the entire collaborative membership (the whole),

although as a policy framework develops, the decision-making should be streamlined. The collaborative needs to spell out what decisions need to be made by the entire membership. In some cases, once the intervention has been designed and implemented, whole system decisions might be limited to decisions that involve money or a certain level of risk to members.

WHO DOES STAFF REPORT TO?

Staff report to the partnership manager or the most senior staff person. The most senior staff person then reports to the collaborative membership as a whole. Over time, the collaborative might streamline reporting roles and responsibilities. If there is policy on this, the reporting goes to the entire membership meeting.

HOW DOES INFORMATION FLOW?

In this organizational form, little information flows between the different parts of the periphery without first going through the centre (see Figure 7). And if a meeting has to facilitate the information flow, a lot of time will be diverted from decision-making. Collaboratives can become more efficient by investing in technology that can easily share information, like websites and or intranets. However, the technology will not make anyone read it. Think about behavioural incentives to get members to read documents before meetings.

Figure 7: Flow of Information in a Democratic Genotype

3. Laissez-faire (Self Organizing) Genotype: Control is vested at the self or action unit

WHO MAKES DECISIONS?

Everyone makes decisions that apply to their own scope of work, but few or no decisions are made collectively and consciously. Saying that, decisions can unconsciously be made collectively, and individuals can make conscious decisions in concert with others that result in tremendous change. The stock market is an example of a laissez-faire genotype. When investors all sell their stock on the same day, the market suffers a loss. But this behaviour is not the result of collective decision-making. No doubt many people could have colluded in back rooms to evoke this reaction, but all the sellers were not involved in decision-making. If your collaborative seems to make decisions but the decisions do not happen in meetings, you might have a laissez-faire situation.

WHO DOES STAFF REPORT TO?

If there is a collaborative manager, then staff would report to him or her. But in a really loose collaborative that is more of a network than a system, it is unlikely that there are any staff directly responsible to the collaborative. Most likely there is a trustee or primary driver, like a municipal government or community development corporation, who manages any resources belonging to the collaborative and acts as the network "hub." There may be an assembly of members at some point, or reporting on an intranet, but the meeting time is more likely taken up with independent project reporting rather than making decisions about the capacity of the collaborative.

HOW DOES INFORMATION FLOW?

Members are tenuously connected to each other and the hub, as shown in Figure 8. In this organizational situation, information may flow sporadically between members if it is necessary to put time and space around the interaction, or may be facilitated speedily through technology like social networks. There is otherwise very little connection between members on a day-to-day basis. However, should a common cause arise that unites members, the potential for concerted advocacy is great. The busier the member organizations are on other foci, the less potential for successful intent interaction.

If any governance is required, it might take the form of rules of interaction on email forums or Internet forums.

Figure 8: Flow of Information in a Laissez-Faire Genotype

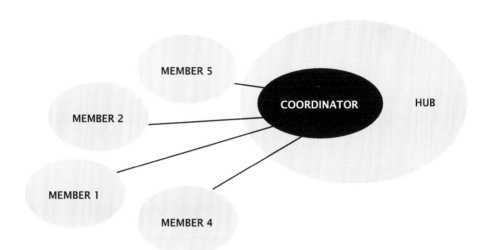

Governance Structure with Sponsor or Trustee

In the case of any of the genotypes described above, you may find the situation where the collaborative engages in a relationship with a trustee to secure funding. Because of the special responsibilities trustees take on to provide financial oversight to collaboratives and their status as an incorporated body, they have a special position of power. It may be a relationship of first amongst equals, but their reputation is on the line by assuming the responsibility to funnel the money to you. They are given a special position near the top of any chart to denote their special role. This responsibility pertains not only to their staff in the form of the executive director, but also applies to the trustee's board of directors.

If your organization has a trustee, add this box to the top of your governance chart!

Governance Structure with a Community Base

Some collaboratives, especially those that are trying to bring about community-wide change, choose to ground their work by sharing power with community members who are not a part of the collaborative's organizational members. Theoretically, all non-profit collaboratives have a responsibility to the broader community, although many choose to reflect it through their own agency boards and membership bases. Since membership bases are usually more numerous than organizational members, place them at the bottom of the chart. This is in line with visual depictions of voters in a representational democracy, assuming the community base comes together infrequently at an annual forum or AGM.

If your organization has a community base, add this box to the bottom of your governance chart!

Although most of this book is focused on the message that governance is a function and must be assumed by the leadership of collaborative, this chapter has explored the explicit process of designing the governance structure for a collaborative. The chapter examined many factors that go into the thoughtful design of a governance and organizational structure, including power, unique needs, areas for decision-making, the specifics of staffing organizational charts, and the three basic genotypes that determine the underlying nature and approach to power sharing for your collaborative.

This chapter also explored the possibilities for a collaborative organizational and governance structure. Three basic genotypes were described that are suitable for collaborative forms. In addition, the chapter discussed the common situations for collaboratives that have a trustee appointed to oversee the financial stewardship of outside funding and resources, and another situation when an inter-organizational collaborative is accountable to a community base.

CHAPTER 5 STEP 1:
Determining the need for a collaborative and exploring the problem set

If the only tool you have is a hammer, you tend to see every problem as a nail.
—Abraham Maslow

Chapter 5 explores Step 1 in the six-step development model for successful collaboratives. As Step 1 deals with defining the problem, the chapter focuses on the difficult nature of problems called *social messes* or complex problems. The chapter also introduces tools to scope out the complex problems that are appropriate for a collaborative response. Although this step is often undertaken by one person or a small group, governance considerations begin to surface at this step. The chapter identifies the themes that emerge throughout the development process. Finally, the chapter introduces systems thinking and concludes with thinking tools to determine when a collaborative is the appropriate course of action.

The first stage begins with the organizing issue or problem set. Spending time at this stage will help clarify the purpose of the entire process and determine its potential as a collaborative. Many NPO leaders feel frustrated at their lack of success in building collaborative endeavours. Proper planning and preparation increase the odds of success and lay the groundwork for open and honest conversation about needs and motivation. What kind of issues prompt people to look to other organizations for help? Steps 1 and 2 are strategic thinking and planning questions for conveners and members to consider prior to joining or starting a collaborative initiative.

Because the complexity of the problem motivates the initial convener to begin the process, we need to look at the dynamics of the problem set to ascertain what can be gained by collaborating with others. Complexity comes from the number of people involved in decision-making, unrealistic expectations regarding time and other factors, and the ongoing pressure from technology. You need to discern whether collaboration can reduce these variables or just enhance their impact.

Building a collaborative requires more time, energy, and resources than those required for a traditional organization. Because of the extra capacity building and the interpersonal and intercultural issues that arise, I urge collaborative members to engage in thoughtful assessment of the problem and the resources needed prior to entering into this time-intensive process.

What problems are unsolvable by a lone organization?
Russell Ackoff, one of the originators of systems thinking, calls the intractable problem sets we face in our chaotic environment *meta problems* and *messes*. Meta problems are the set of all problems that make up a single problem—the one you have to solve. In contrast, messes are *not* merely problems. Problems have solutions; messes do not have straightforward solutions.

Social messes:

- are more than complicated and complex—they are ambiguous;

- contain considerable uncertainty, even in terms of what the conditions are, let alone what the appropriate actions might be;

- are bounded by great constraints and are tightly interconnected economically, socially, politically, and technologically;

- are seen differently from different points of view, and quite different worldviews;

- contain many value conflicts; and

- are often a-logical or illogical. (Horn, 2001, p. 1)

Messes are the meta-problems of drugs and gangs, ethnic conflict, and intransigent problems like homelessness and poverty. It is no surprise to those of us who work for social change that these messes are our issues! Messes are strongly linked to impacts of globalization, civil wars, international population shifts, and the rapid advance of technology.

Brenda Zimmerman, a complexity researcher at York University, has developed a way of looking at and categorizing problems. She finds there are basically three types of problems characterized by the nature of the required solutions.

Table 2: The Nature and Conceptualization of Problems

SIMPLE	COMPLICATED	COMPLEX
Solution example: Following a recipe to bake a cake	**Building a rocket to get to the moon**	**Raising a child to become an effective member of society**
• The recipe is essential	• Formulae are critical and necessary	• Formulae have only a limited application
• Recipes are tested to assure replication of later efforts	• Sending one rocket increases assurance that next will be okay	• Raising one child gives no assurance of success with the next
• No particular expertise; knowing how to cook increases success	• High level of expertise in many specialized fields + coordination	• Expertise can help but is not sufficient; relationships are key
• Recipe notes the quantity and nature of "parts" needed	• Separate into parts and then coordinate	• Can't separate parts from the whole
• Recipes produce standard products	• Rockets are similar in critical ways	• Every child is unique

Adapted from a presentation to the Joint Canadian Evaluation Society/American Evaluation Association Conference,Toronto, October 29, 2005. *Simple, Complicated and Complex Problem Framings and the Implications for Evaluation*, Brenda Zimmerman, Schulich School of Business, York University, Toronto, Canada.

When we apply this conceptual framework to the collaboration field, it is obvious that what Ackoff called m*eta problems* and *messes* (Ackoff, 1981) and what Zimmerman calls *complex problems* and others are calling *wicked problems* (Innes & Booher, p. 10), are not easily solved through a recipe or a fixed formula. These types of problems need a change agent who is oriented outside of their organization. The Sanskrit word *Ashima* (endless, limitless, boundaryless) is sometimes used to describe complex or wicked problems; this is the territory where ambiguity reigns. Since not even the problem is clear, much time is needed to build common understanding and to determine where there is power and energy to make change. Complex problems need a mechanism that can accommodate the cross-boundary ownership of the issues and the multiple players needed to make change.

Throughout the process, boundary negotiation is constant—boundaries around the problem, the boundary around the system, and interpersonal boundaries between members—thereby needing a lot of decision-making activity. The mechanism often used to discover the problem and develop solutions is a collaborative with a decision-making process and governance structure. Building an understanding of the whole picture to mobilize new understanding and additional resources becomes the motivation to collaborate with outside organizations.

These questions will help you distinguish a mess from a simple problem:

1. Who are the players?

2. Who has responsibility or ownership of the problem?

3. What are the individual problems?

4. What are current initiatives to address the problems?

5. What are the causes of the individual problems?

6. What are the constraints or barriers to building solutions?

7. What might be the underlying systemic issues?

8. What are the values and motivations of the system participants?

A collaboration may be a good problem solving strategy when several stakeholders have a vested interest in the problem and are willing to work together developing solutions. A collaborative is even more appropriate if there is a history of incremental or sporadic efforts to deal with the problem set that have not produced satisfactory solutions, and the problem seems to be unsolvable or exasperatingly persistent.

If there is a history of single organizations failing to develop sustainable solutions and partners are willing to collaborate, then you can move forward confidently. Each member brings their predetermined analysis and probable solutions to the table. Preferred solutions need to be put aside until the opportunity to explore the problem set is worked through the different perspectives of collaborative members.

Tools to Scope out the Problem
All members of the collaboration eventually need to have the same mental model of the mess or complex problem. Prior to even asking people to join together, it is prudent to explore the problem set. Problem exploration tools include environmental scanning, scenario building, and literature reviews.

Environmental Scans:
A scan is a conscious action of identifying trends and emerging developments. Trend scanning can be as informal as a group exercise, or as formal as a well-funded trend monitoring system, with an ongoing network of people, a

wide range of information resources, and regular publications. It is best to do environmental scanning frequently on a weekly or daily basis to provide yourself with constantly updated information about emerging threats and opportunities.

Typical scan questions include the following:

- Who else is doing what you do?

- How are others doing what you do?

- What is happening in all levels of government with the issues that affect your client group?

- What are the government's priorities in terms of social policy generally and in your sector?

- How does the government view the non-profit sector?

- What new legislation might affect your work or your client group?

- Is there competition with what you do?

- Are there ways of working more cheaply?

- What new technology is on the horizon that might affect the work you do?

- What is happening with respect to labour relations in your sector in general?

- Does your workforce have the skills and competencies to deliver the programming needed?

Boundary spanning, a term used to describe the competency of environmental scanning, is now seen as principal job function of an executive director. However, this can be an important function for all board members and staff in various team configurations. Collective intelligence gathered by a team, that is shared and analyzed, can be more extensive and thorough and produce a more thoughtful overview of what is happening in the external environment. It can also contribute to the use of the next tool.

Scenario Building:
Scenario planning is a tool whereby the planner connects the dots (pieces of data) gleaned from the external environment and walks through the implications of these dots on the system—be it an organization, sector, or community. The planner

notices a trend and then imagines the impact on and possibilities for the planner's own organization or an issue. Scenarios are stories rather than a prediction. Positive and negative possibilities can happen; this leads to the terms worst case and best case scenarios.

You never know when opportunity can arise out of a bad situation. To most of us, a forest fire is a pretty bad scenario; but not to certain types of beetles. Some beetles have special infrared receptors that can detect the heat from a forest fire. When they discover the aftermath of a forest fire, they move right in and lay their eggs in the forest. They know that when the eggs hatch, the larvae can feed off of the dead wood.

In the world of nature there are countless examples of how good comes from something we perceive as bad. I suppose it is only bad because we want something other than the result we got. When we look at a situation calmly and sum up what is really going on, perhaps there is really some good in it and we can use this to our advantage.

(Source: Bleckmann, H.J., Schmitz, H., & von der Emde, G. Nature as a model for technical sensors, *J. Comp. Physiol. A.*, 190:971–981, 2004.)

Thinking through possible scenarios alone or with others is a key strategic thinking and leadership skill set for finding solutions to complex problems. By considering scenarios that might emerge, key development questions will emerge and you can consider possible answers, such as who holds the puzzle pieces needed to explore the problem and who might be good members for a collaborative approach to problem solving.

For a comprehensive learning guide to scenario building for non-profit organizations, download: *What if? The art of scenario thinking for non-profits* from www.gbn.com/whatif.

Literature Review:
NPO practitioners are increasingly initiating planning for new programs or interventions with a review of the academic literature. A literature review can also become the knowledge foundation or a jumping off point for a group learning process. If a report scans and succinctly presents the existing knowledge and perspectives on a problem set, it can help all members of a collaborative to quickly get up to speed on the topic.

A literature review is a way to:

- compare studies and know "what's out there" on a specific topic;

- analytically examine an existing body of research;

- identify an article that documents a particular fact; and

- bring order out of too much information spread across too many places.

There are many reasons for doing a literature review, such as:

- putting your work in context and knowing what others are doing;

- discovering best practices and worst nightmares;

- supporting and justifying grant proposals, new programs, interventions, evaluations, presentations, and staff development;

- giving your work credibility; and

- fulfilling intellectual and personal curiosities.

One last word on gathering information on the complex issue: it is quite possible that there is little information to gather in the academic literature. If in-depth studying of a problem could lead to a satisfactory solution, someone would probably have done it and written about it. But most complex problems are highly political, thereby not lending themselves to simple solutions. People who work in politically-charged situations (just about everyone in the NPO sector or government) rarely take the time to reflect and record what worked. However, almost everyone will stop for few minutes and talk with you. If you need guidance, take the opportunity to arrange individual interviews with collaborative leaders or experts. They may even be grateful for the opportunity to reflect on what they have learned.

Governance Considerations

Who has the power to make decisions at this step?

I will look at sources of power later on, but those working through the questions listed above have to consider where their legitimacy to act is coming from. You do not need to stop what you are doing, but if you are making decisions, you need to consider by what authority you can act. For example:

- Are you a concerned citizen using the power to act that comes with your residency in a community?

- Are you working for an institution or an organization that has a mission to address the problem?

- Are you empowered by a government to address the issue?

Organization development theorists and psychologists use the term agency to describe someone who steps up to the plate and does something to react to an issue. This type of human behaviour is not enacted as often as we need it to be. It is wonderful then someone decides to act with a sense of agency. It needs to be a conscious decision, but also a thoughtful one, because once you step up you are shaking the existing order and people will question your motivation and ambitions. You become a threat to the existing system. Your main decision at this point may simply be to act and invite others to join you in the process. All other decisions can be made with others, thereby giving the process the legitimacy or authority of its members.

Defining the Problem

You or your organization may be undertaking literature reviews, opening files, and writing reports on the issue. Your perspective on the problem may be coloured by your institutional mental models that you continue to put forward. This perspective is flawed, or else the problem would be solved. You must let it go and let others share their perspective before the problem is even defined. Using the land use planning/exploration metaphor suggested earlier: Christopher Columbus thought he was in China when landing in the new world for the first time. Because he was looking for spices, he could not see the new resources of maize and timber until he was there long enough to realize he was in a new place altogether, and he needed to use what was under his nose.

You too are in new territory and need to be open to the new knowledge and ways of seeing the problem that others will bring. You can share the information and knowledge gleaned so far and use it as starting place upon which to build the collective understanding of the problem. By inviting others into the process, you let go of the power to control how the problem is defined and create the space for a new system to emerge.

Systems Awareness: What are systems?

When used in the context of people and organizations, a system is a group of people with a common purpose. Organizations, governments, and families are all systems. However, crowds or audiences are not systems as they do not work together on a common cause. Systems have a history, a character, and distinctive competencies.

A system includes the following parts: input, process, output, with a feedback loop and a boundary. Figure 9 shows this process.

Figure 9: Parts of a System

Everything—from atoms, to people, to organizations, to nations, to the Universe—operates as a system. Things go in, things are transformed, and things come out. Feedback is generated. Feedback is used. Boundaries define, differentiate, and connect/interface. An existing system may be responsible for the problem set you are considering. Scoping out the existing system may help you explore the complex problem. Systems thinking helps you to explore what is lurking below the surface of an issue or problem.

Systems are not closed, however, but operate in their environment. In non-profit organizations, senior managers can spend as much time managing up into the environment as down into the service delivery (tasks like advocacy and fundraising). This environmental management is part of the interdependency between non-profit organizations and the larger political and social system. If you use your organization as an example, you can observe it operating in an environment that includes government, funders, stakeholders, clients, and other agencies and sectoral organizations (see Figure 10). When looking at a complex problem, you will find it is situated in a chaotic environment where there is change and/or inertia and unsupportive energy. By collaborating with others and by building a trans-organizational system, you hope to calm that external turmoil by exhorting more influence over that environment.

Figure 10: An Organization's Environment

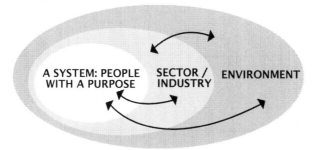

> **When the system makes plans in reaction to change in the environment then the actions of the system can change the environment.**

Existing Service Systems are a Mess!

The human service delivery system has evolved without conscious planning in most of North America. It now finds itself embroiled in a value system conflict with its funders. NPOs operate with independent missions and often with few resources to fulfill their goals, whereas funders are concerned with the broader service system and fear service duplication and redundancy. To prevent these threats, in the last 15 years funders have built a competitive funding framework that encourages a survival of the fittest dynamic. This framework results in a low wage structure, which prevents retention and quality—major systems issue now that that baby boom generation is retiring.

Leaders engaged in governance roles in NPO organizations or collaboratives need to have a systems understanding to help address complex problems. I often coach executive directors who spend their time putting band-aids on systemic problems, all the while blaming themselves and giving up what little free time they have. Complex systemic problems require systemic solutions. Band-aids only perpetuate the system, bringing the problem back to the way it was rather than changing it.

Should our organization work with external organizations?

As one member of the larger system, consider how much power and influence you have to change the system. You may be a large NPO with close to ties to bureaucracy and government. Do you need the power and/or legitimacy of other agencies and departments with a common position to be able to speak on behalf of a sector?

It almost always makes sense to aggregate the political power of separate organizations when trying to influence a political system. However, many funders are now trying to foster closer ties between members of a human delivery system, and are providing funding to develop collaboratively-run programs. NPO leaders express the greatest frustration with these experiments. Funders are using collaboration as a code term for system rationalization (Graham, 2007), and NPOs get involved only with trepidation. However, collaboratives make the most sense when they help the individual NPO achieve a larger scale to acquire efficiencies or buying power (e.g., when three agencies pool their resources to hire a human resource specialist, or to form a purchasing collaborative to do bulk buying). In this way, NPOs can jointly achieve the scale necessary to buy goods and services unavailable to a small organization.

When a collaborative is not appropriate?

I worked for one organization whose mission statement celebrated that they do all their work in partnership. While this is a nice sentiment, it is not an efficient approach for any organization. When a single organization can manage the intervention or program by itself, it should. Avoid the investment in time and energy in working across cultures if it is clear that there is no value proposition to collaborating with others.

A collaborative is also not appropriate when there is no time or resources to devote to building the organizational capacity necessary for success. Small organizations often turn to collaboration as a strategy for organizational survival. It usually does not work. The executive director often ends up attending numerous external meetings to position the collaborative as legitimate and eligible for funding, meanwhile neglecting the home organization and programs. It is a far better use of senior leadership's time to build your internal organizational capacity and build relationships on behalf of your own organization. When your own house is in order, then it is time to engage in collaboration. Otherwise, you will just bring your organizational chaos with you to the collaborative.

When a collaborative is proposed by external funders but is not aligned with grassroots needs, it is not appropriate. As mentioned earlier, when you chase the money, you enable the funding system to believe collaboration is the best tool to achieve system rationalization.

Finally, when there is no track record of cooperation amongst potential members, but rather a long history of inter-organizational conflict and anticipated competition, a collaborative is not the best option. One systemic impact of the competitive funding framework is that NPOs have to compete against each other. Competition stimulates aggressive behaviour, leading to deteriorated relationships. Can you guess how much time it will take to repair a bitter relationship? Is there enough time and money to do so? If not, walk away.

PRELIMINARY CHECKLIST TO DETERMINE APPROPRIATENESS OF A COLLABORATIVE:

- What are you most qualified to offer to address the identified problems?

- Is anyone else already doing what you can do? If so, do you have anything to add?

- In the areas where you are qualified, where can you make the most significant difference? Where will you have the most leverage?

- What are the pros and cons of intervening in this way?

- Will this make the best use of the resources you have available? Is it worth the opportunity cost?

Step 1 is only the beginning of the collaborative journey. It could end at any moment if you realize that it is a journey not worth taking. If you keep finding reasons to proceed and see that doors are opening, make as few decisions as possible; you are just laying the foundation at this point. Explore the problem, but do not define it. Keep your mind open and explore your own and your organization's mental models so that others can join you in the exploration.

CHAPTER 6 STEP 2:
Motivation to Act

Go to your bosom: Knock there, and ask your heart what it doth know.
— William Shakespeare

This chapter explores one of the drivers of collaboration that of organizational and personal self-interest. For people to contribute their ideas and resources and be willing to change, they must be motivated. As a practitioner, you need to use many ways to motivate people to take on new tasks and grow into new change agent roles. This chapter discusses what it means to be social entrepreneur and what to reflect on if you are taking on the responsibility for convening a new collaborative. Governance issues also emerge at the motivation to collaborate stage. At this stage, it is prudent to map out your own interest and the interest of potential partners. In addition, this chapter begins to explore the pitfalls of mandated or incented collaborations where funders require collaboration as a pre-condition for funding a sectoral or community initiative.

Motivation involves the desire to achieve a task and the willingness to carry it out. Collaborative processes do not gain momentum unless potential participants see a benefit from the investment of their time and energy. The task of exploring a complex problem set, sharing knowledge, and building a common vision is an especially difficult one. Everyone involved needs to be highly motivated to engage in the process.

In the Inter-Agency Services Collaboration Project (IASCP), we found that the motivation and perception of benefit for many organizations in the NPO sector comes with the difficulty of dealing with complex social issues or addressing gaps in service delivery. In one of the reports, *The East Scarborough Storefront Project: A Successful Inter-Organizational Service Collaboration*, the notion of "overwhelming need" motivated the initial community agencies and community activists to collaborate. A new population of refugees with few supports moved into short-term housing in this suburban community, and the need for services was so apparent that community members mobilized and invited existing agencies to collaborate to provide services. Due to dramatic funding cuts to the NPO sector in 1999, the project leadership considered development of a new agency impossible.

Motivation to collaborate emerged as a critical element in another IASC project, *The Korean Interagency Network (KIN)* process. Participants keenly expressed their anxiety over the sustainability of their organizations and concern over their community's equitable access to public resources. Participants and observers noted that mainstream and larger organizations that were members of KIN did not feel compelled to participate. Many thought that they did not share the same issues that motivated the other participants to collaborate.

Self-Interest

Prior to even asking anybody to come to a table, collaborative leaders would be wise to map out their interests and the interests of potential partners. Although we uphold the value of altruism in the human service sector, we must acknowledge the role of self-interest in terms of any form of participation. If you do any form of volunteer recruitment, you know that people volunteer for more than altruistic reasons. Whether to gain valuable work experience, meet requirements for education reasons, or make new friends, there needs to something in it for them to motivate them to honour their commitment to show up and do what they promised.

Yet frequently when human service providers come to a collaborative table, they use words like:

- *Let's do this for the client.*

- *If this is good for the client, then it's good for my agency.*

- *Let's put all our petty squabbles aside and focus on moving forward.*

Then a few months down the road, intense conflict breaks out and all the goodwill flies out the window. Since the process is not based on honesty, people walk away. It does no good to talk about the real issues.

What are the real issues? Well, what is seen to be good for the client is often what is good for one agency over another. At least one organization is getting what it needs out the process and others are not. The issue might be defining the problem or mess in light of one particular approach that favours the service delivery approach of one partner, or can be further down the road in terms of who gets what piece of funding or the bulk of back office support. Game theory, used in probability software, predicts that with a group of nine players the possible issues for conflict number over a half million.

The opportunities for dissension are high. No one can predict what topic will submerge the collaborative process. However, by creating a climate of openness where partners can discuss what they need out of the process and what motivates them to participate and stay in the process, you increase the chances that whenever one of those half million issues emerges, you can talk about it in an open and frank manner.

Individuals have Self-Interest Too!

Not only do organizations have interests, but people have self-interest too. In one of the literature searches for the IASCP, the most substantiated benefit of collaboration was the benefit to an individual's career. By participating in a collaborative, people made new contacts and were able to pursue new career opportunities. Never forget that individuals represent the organizational members and bring their gifts, needs, and talents to the process. They can be enthusiastic or sabotage the whole process. Pay attention to these ways to motivate your members, listed in Table 3, if you are a partnership manager.

Table 3: Ways to Motivate People

an important goal	building their self-esteem	being around positive people
appreciation for work well done	building their self-respect	products and services they believe in
personal and family values	informal interaction	positive surprises
respecting their contribution	open doors	public acclaim
future opportunity	personal plans	a sincere "thank you"
an inspirational leader	career paths	being "known" by important people
a positive work environment	a variety of experiences	their identity on their work
competition	educational opportunities	valuing their ideas
being part of a team	a bonus	

Table 3: Ways to Motivate People

performance standards	chance to "own" something	asking them for help
deadlines	self-direction	a chance to create
quotas	ego	involvement
recognition awards	performance reviews	self-expression
identifying with something important	professionalism	security
internal/company announcements	open communications	a well-defined plan
public announcements	feedback	encouragement
gifts	high expectations	company accomplishments
flexible work hours	feeling needed	time off
fears	feeling valued	a trip
a challenge	feeling important	choice
monetary rewards	opportunity to grow	basic benefits
pride	a new start	experience success
loyalty	a positive change	inspirational quotes
self-interest	additional responsibility	honest/candid relationship
a vision of the future	company image	telling them you're counting on them

Social Entrepreneurs

Academics are looking closely at the initiator of collaborative processes and call them collaborative entrepreneurs (Takahashi & Smutny, 2002). Similar to the life cycle theory of organizations (both for-profit and non-profit) that requires an entrepreneur during the start-up phase of an organization, researchers are starting to identify a similar role in the life cycle of collaborative. This delineation between entrepreneur and manager happens infrequently in the life cycle of NPOs. More commonly, social entrepreneurs start up a new NPO, stick around in the CEO function, and run it badly. When they leave the organization has to grapple with "founders syndrome," a situation where the founder dominated decision-making and the culture of the organization.

As with traditional organizations, the collaborative entrepreneur recognizes a need that presents an opportunity for change. Researchers call this need a *collaborative window.* More importantly, collaborative entrepreneurs with a sense of agency and an awareness of their own motivation to act, have the capacity and networks to bring together relevant, important, and appropriate stakeholders and participants. That same person may not be highly effective at maintaining, sustaining, or adapting particular partnerships to changing conditions as collaborative windows close (Takahashi & Smutny, 2002). So, the collaborative entrepreneur and the collaboration manager may be different people in the process. The terms *entrepreneur* and *manager* are useful to understand the difference in function, but the term convener is used more to describe the initial leadership role in perusing the collaborative window and calling people together in the NPO and government sectors in North America.

The Convening Role

This role is one of the most difficult roles of an NPO leader. You can be a good manager, but a terrible convener. Whereas a manager or a director has the ability to use coercive power to motivate people to assume work tasks, the convener of a collaborative has no formal authority over other members. Influence and persuasion skills are needed, and the process of enrolling people to sign onto a new collaborative venture can feel like having one's teeth pulled. A convener has to summon up the vision and enthusiasm to act as a counterforce to NPO leaders who are overwhelmed with paperwork and needs, to respond on a moment's notice to what seem to be irrational decisions like cutbacks and administrivia requirements by decision-makers. A convener's personal leadership style needs to be more lateral in nature than the leadership style needed in hierarchical organizations. And yes, most NPOs are still organized hierarchically because their funders require it. However, according to one source, since so much NPO work focuses on building relationships, public sector managers may have a leg up on their private sector counterparts (IBM Global Business Services, 2006, p. 24).

The principal task of a convener is to recruit the members of the potential collaborative. The convener can be one person or can be members of a steering committee. The invitation to participate needs to address the issue of motivation and benefits to collaborating. When enrolling participants, conveners need to identify and work with the self-interest of their target members. This sets a tone of authenticity and honesty to establish a collaborative of mutual benefit. Since the collaborative has no structure to begin with, the convener and members establish a process of co-creating a new organizational structure (a trans-organizational system). However, self-interest does not lead to the development of a common purpose for a new collaborative. If the collaborative is formed to seek a funding opportunity, as we saw earlier, people will take the money and form a collaborative in name only. Then they will go back to what they were doing before. An appeal to higher ideals and the common good is necessary to sustain the work over the long term and develop the complex solutions to social messes that come from commitment and hard work.

A convener may assume the chairing role once meetings start, but this does not need to happen automatically. Someone must assume the coordination activities of organizing and scheduling the first meeting; the convener or convening committee usually assumes that responsibility. Whether the convener continues to provide coordination or leadership is an issue the group needs to decide early on in the process. Some personality types are really good networkers and are able to bring diverse people and organizations together. However, they have poor coordination and management skills and thereby fail to undertake the ongoing coordination needed to keep up the momentum of an emerging group. Groups are wise to discuss the issue and find ways to complement the skills of its members, rather than assume the person who called the initial meeting will do all the support work from then on. I will explore the process of identifying and selecting those desired members in Step 3.

Another role that the convener takes on is that of champion. This is a leadership function rather than one of governance. Many leadership experts see this role or aspect of leadership as necessary to make large system changes. These experts think that a leader is necessary to develop a vision of a desired future or a solution to the problem, and to communicate it to inspire others to join in and implement the vision. A well-communicated problem definition and possibilities for a common strategy are definitely necessary to convince participants to join a collaborative process. However, if there is no opportunity to explore the problem and discuss strategies and solutions that incorporate members' perspectives, the collaborative will not survive. A collaborative has the potential to function democratically as members each have one vote or the power to vote with their feet and disengage.

When pulling people together, conveners should champion the collaborative, not their personal vision. There is power in defining the problem and defining the appropriate solutions. When one person's (or organization's) interpretation and ideas get all the say, others shy away.

Lubricating the mechanisms of the group mind so that it can think and act brilliantly demands emotional intelligence. (Goleman, 1998)

Consider the following reflection questions before taking on the convening role:

1. Does addressing the issue fall within the mission and mandate of your organization?

2.   What might be the outcome on your clients? Would they get better service?

3   Can your agency/department develop a program without the help of other organizations? Do you have the skills and funding?

4 . Is a collaborative process the best mechanism to formulate a solution to the issue?

5   Is there enough good will and trust amongst potential members to overcome the tension of being competitors at times?

6.   What is the likelihood of other organizations getting involved? Do they care about the issue? Do they have a mandate to address it?

7.   Is there competition for other organizations' time and attention? Is a big event or transition coming up that might deflect time and resources from the focus of the collaborative?

8.   Do you and/or your staff have the time available to devote to this process?

9.   Will potential funders look upon the collaborative favourably?

10. What possible interventions would address the problem set? What combination of agencies/people and skills are needed to support the possible interventions?

11. What might be some possible benefits to your organization, your sector, and/ or community? What kinds of challenges might emerge?

Once you answer these questions, you will have a better understanding of the likelihood of success. If the answers do not show overwhelming benefits and possible support from potential members, consider alternatives such as laying a foundation of trust building or waiting for better conditions to emerge.

Personal Commitment

Because of their potential for power sharing, collaboratives are a different kind of organization than workplaces. Participating and leading in a collaborative require different skills and leadership approaches. This is not always apparent to all members, and unless there is open and honest communication about expectations around leadership and participation, most people revert to what they know. In our society, employees and managers know best how to behave in hierarchical organizations, often where the boss is treated as a supreme ruler because of the coercive power and formal authority that come with the position of manager. In a collaborative—formed on a voluntary basis where no-one has coercive power, when everyone around the table is a volunteer—traditional leadership skills such as providing direction and communicating expectations can alienate others. Instead, a style called *lateral leadership* is more appropriate. I will revisit this topic throughout the book.

Governance Issues at the Motivation to Collaborate Stage

There are real governance and power considerations that the convener or convening committee should explore before beginning the meeting process. It is wise to map the interest of potential partners working in the problem area. First, brainstorm a list of organizations and stakeholders engaged in the area of work. This list may be really long or quite brief, depending on the problem domain. If there are more than 35 stakeholders, start to identify representative organizations such as sector organizations or existing coalitions. The more thorough you are at this step, the more thoughtful you can be in the member selection stage. Next, fill in their names in a chart like the one below (Table 4). Write down as many details about the stakeholder as you can identify. If you are unaware of the organization, check its webpage and then begin an informal data gathering process by asking colleagues about the organization.

Table 4: Chart of Potential Partners

NAME OF STAKE-HOLDER	MISSION	CURRENT INTEREST IN THE PROBLEM DOMAIN	UNIQUE ASSETS	MISCEL-LANEOUS	LIKELY TO PARTICIPATE

Mission: Check the agency's website to find its mission.
Current interest in the problem domain: What program does it deliver in this area? Has it engaged in any research on the topic? Does it have staff or board members with an interest in the area?

Unique assets: Does this organization have access to a population or community that is vital to a future strategy? Are any staff knowledgeable of the target area?

Miscellaneous: Do you have any baggage with this organization? Are there competitive issues with your organization or others? Do you have a piece of intelligence that could be vital or that could impact the success of a future collaborative?

Likely to participate: After identifying its mission and interest, and assessing its motivation, can you say whether the organization is likely to be interested in participating?

These stakeholders are not necessarily the partners you will invite to join the collaborative, although it is likely some of them will be. You can save a lot of time at this stage by being strategic (e.g., if you discover that most of the stakeholders are too busy to engage in a new initiative or would prefer limited involvement).

Forced or Incented Collaboration
Sometimes funders want learning transfer (and maybe the development of closer ties that will lead to some form of merger) to take place between large organizations and smaller or emerging ones, and initiate a funder program to foster these type of collaborations. These are often very weak collaboratives, as it is not often in the small agency's interest to participate as its very existence and mission is at risk. As a survival strategy, it cooperates to get the money and stay on the good side of funders, but usually subverts any relationship from developing.

In another report for the IASC project, *Service Delivery Collaboration in the Toronto NPO Sector: A Key Informant Survey* by Heather Graham, the respondents reported that mandated collaborations are generally viewed as not sustainable—but not because of the lack of resources. Rather they see mandated collaborations as opportunistic; there is a lack genuine committment to the problem. So, the lesson to funders when they build incented partnership programs is that the fundees only participate to secure the funding, rather than to deal with a complex problem or mess.

In another IASCP report, *Service Delivery Collaboration in Non-profit Health and Community Services: What does Government Want*, author Rob Horwarth discovered a widespread view within government circles (local, provincial and federal) and documented in public reports, that the mechanism of collaboration is used to improve service delivery outcomes. These could include activities such as networking for improved service coordination and the consolidation of services. However, policy supports to facilitate inter-organization collaboration are few and exist primarily at the municipal level. Most importantly, provincial supports do not exist, even though this is the level of government where NPOs receive 80% of their funding to provide community-based health and social services.

Throughout the IASCP research process, respondents reported their suspicion of the motivation of funders when they develop collaboration funding programs. Without support to build the inter-organizational capacity needed to address the complexities of collaboration, and with the government's veiled efforts to downsize and streamline delivery systems, NPOs and funders seem to be working at cross purposes. The IASCP reports documented the commitment to tackling difficult social issues, despite the lack of funding for bottom-up initiatives and the lack of capacity in the NPO sector. Many NPOs continue to embark on new collaborative ventures to tackle the social messes that they are mandated to address. Within that commitment, it always takes one person in one organization to say, "Let's step outside of our organizational boundaries and work with others to find a new strategy for this complex problem." This person, if empowered to go forward, assumes the convening role.

Initiators of the process do so because they are motivated to act. You need to understand those motivators, and then determine the motivations of potential members. By accepting that self-interest is a principal motivator at the beginning, you can help move the collaborative toward common ground at a later stage. Moving outside of your organization's walls can be the beginning of a leadership journey. The roles and skills required are different than those required in a traditional government or NPO workplace. Examining your own motivation is the foundation for building the motivation to collaborate.

CHAPTER 7 STEP 3:
Member Identification—Who should belong?

Knowledge has to be improved, challenged, and increased constantly, or it vanishes.—Peter Drucker

Step 3 is the member identification and recruitment stage, where political dynamics emerge and need to be considered. Who gets to come to the table can be a highly political process, or the process can be at the opposite end of the spectrum: a situation where no-one wants to engage at all. However, it is critical to remember that member selection always involves recruiting knowledge resources into the process. This chapter explores ways of getting the right people into the process, including the convener. This includes using criteria for member selection to ensure a complementary mix of knowledge and resources or access to populations or markets, and selecting members who can act on behalf of their agency. Potential members need become thoughtful and strategic as they accept or reject invitations to participate. This chapter also begins to explore the key governance issue of dealing with power and turf issues while working across organizational boundaries.

All organizations are knowledge repositories and do knowledge work!
Peter Drucker[11] coined the concept of the knowledge organization and the knowledge worker in the mid-20th century. Instead of seeing the modern organization as a machine as did prior management theorists, he saw it as a brain that processed information into knowledge. Information was the input

---

[11] Peter Drucker is one of the foremost management theorists of the 20th century. In 1959, Drucker coined the term "knowledge worker," and he authored Managing the *Non-Profit Organization: Practices and Principles in* 1990.

and knowledge the output of the modern organization. His views of modern organizations that apply to collaboratives are as follows:

1. Organizations must have a *system principle* or a reason for being—a purpose. In the case of a family, the system principle is to provide emotional and financial support and/or raise children. In the case of a non-profit organization, the mission is to provide service or education. In a business, the system principle is the provision of goods or services for profit. A collaborative must have a system principle or a purpose as well.

2. Organizations manage knowledge to achieve desired results. Knowledge is a critical mass of information looked at through the lens of experience and critical thinking, which enables us to predict and control something. Collaboratives are also a means to assemble knowledge.

3. Organizations are comprised of knowledge specialists and generalists who manage the interface between knowledge specialties. Bits of knowledge by themselves are sterile. They become productive only if welded together into a useful body of knowledge. The organization's central task is to make this transformation of knowledge possible. In other words, the organization's work is to add value to incoming information gleaned from its workers, its customers/clients, and its environment, and then transform this into the output of a service or product. If there is not a value-added process or transformation, then there is no work and no authentic organization. In the case of a family, the transformation of knowledge results in meeting the emotional and financial needs of family members.

4. A collaborative (trans-organizational system) also manages knowledge. Knowledge must be managed in a similar fashion to any organization comprised of specialists. However, instead of employee specialists, the member organizations are the knowledge specialists. The specialist knowledge is not necessarily the knowledge of an academic discipline, but can also be the voice of lived experience by a particular constituency. In the case of an NPO, this can be its knowledge of service provision to its client base. The knowledge inputs needed depend on the analysis of the problem by the process convener, and who the convener (might be a convening committee) identifies as a potential member of the collaborative. Therein lies the fatal flaw of the whole process: those who get to play in the game determine the eventual direction of the outcome. As computer engineers say, "garbage in and garbage out" (GIGO). The saying is commonly used to describe failures in human decision making due to faulty, incomplete, or imprecise data.

The purpose of a collaborative is to create and implement a strategy to solve a complex problem. The work process is one of continuous learning, decision-making, and then implementation of those decisions. If the knowledge resources invited to participate in the process provide incomplete or inaccurate data, the decisions and new knowledge (incorporated into a plan) will not be effective.

By the 1990s, it was becoming evident to academics that the growth in task scope for organizations was overwhelming the internal knowledge resources (Hudson et al, 1999). In the non-profit sector:

> ..society's concepts of 'dysfunction' and 'pathology' are becoming more complex, the incidence of multiple 'problem clients' is increasing, and responses can rarely be confined to only one organization. In such circumstances organizational individualism is seen as inappropriate and inadequate, even where front-line personnel seek to address the problem through informal networks. (Hudson et al, 1999)

Hudson et al also cite work by Huxham and Macdonald (1992) that identifies four types of problems and behaviours that emerged with this growth in task scope. The four pitfalls of individualism include:

1. **Repetition:** where two or more organizations separately carry out an action or task which need only be done by one.

2. **Omission**: where activities which are important to the objectives of more than one organization are not carried out. This may occur because they have not been identified as important, because they come into no organization's remit (mission) or because each organization assumes the other is performing the activity.

3. **Divergence:** the actions of the various organizations may become diffused across a range of activities, rather than used towards common goals.

4. **Counter-pioductioti**[12]**:** organizations working in isolation may take actions which conflict with those taken by others.

Does the activity around your target problems remind you of any of the behaviours identified above? Are there organizations working at cross purposes? Are there so many players in your area of interest that no-one knows what is really happening? Are there gaps in service delivery that permit clients to fall through? You need to explore these knowledge questions as you identify potential members.

---

[12] *pioductioti is an obscure term used in the original text. Substitute productive and you get the gist of what is meant.*

When you assume that the people you are inviting into the process are knowledge resources, it forces you to think and act more intentionally than just "going with the usual suspects." But first convenors need to be conscious of their own motivation and fit for the role of convening.

If you are the convener, are you right for the role?

Extroversion: Do people energize you, or after some time do you find yourself drained and need to be by yourself to wind down?

Networker: Can you meet new people easily, or are you shy and hesitant to approach people you don't know?

Influence and persuasion skills: Since a convener usually has little authority to make people come together (because the potential members are outside of the home organization), you need to be able to enroll people as volunteers into the process. Do people follow you eagerly and enthusiastically? Do you have a good reputation, and do people trust that you will follow through on what you promise?

Control: Do you have the ability to let go of the need to manage and control the process and the eventual outcomes? As you are asking other people and organizations to join you in an exploration of the complex problem and the development of possible strategies, you cannot control the eventual outcomes except by sharing your needs and knowledge.

Political intelligence: Are you aware of power, how it sourced, and how it translates into political dynamics in groups and organizations? Can you talk about self-interest with your potential members and ask them what they need out of the process? Can you negotiate your way through conflicting needs and perspectives?

A convener needs to be a people person, someone who is energized by the process rather than frustrated by it. As the solutions to complex problems are grounded in relationships, conveners need to know that a good part of their role in convening a collaborative is devoted to building and maintaining relationships. You may be a content expert, which gives you credibility with others and motivates them to engage in the process, but your expertise (and ego) will have to be subsumed to the greater task of enrolling others into the process and building an effective group.

This is a critical performance management decision for large institutions that convene multi-stakeholder collaboratives for their programming and intervention strategies. In my experience, many public health units initiate health-focused collaboratives as part of provincial policy and programs with technically trained health service providers who may not be a good fit for the role of convener. A practitioner trained for and comfortable with one-on-one interaction may not be comfortable with managing large group dynamics and the politics that emerge with member organizations. Collaborative development has to be entered into voluntarily because it requires term energy, stamina, and infinite patience.

Getting the Right People into the Process

A convener or convening committee has to decide what factors need to be addressed and which are important to potential members. In the NPO sector, the most common strategy is to recruit "the usual suspects." You need to be more thoughtful when selecting members and look at potential members as a resource to help address the social mess or complex issue. Of course, the problem dictates the framework; or, as architects say, form follows function. If the collaborative is an advocacy coalition formed to address the actions of a common funder, at first glance all the fundees are the most likely members of the coalition to change funding rules. However, even then it would be strategic to broaden the membership to include others—maybe clients of the programs, other agencies that refer to the program, faith groups, or community-based organizations that intersect with the funded programs. If the organization issue is a complex problem or social mess, your selection of members process should take this into account and you should devote the time needed to analyze potential contributors.

Consider the following factors as criteria for member selection:

- Does the issue affect the population they serve?

- Can the potential organization bring unique knowledge and perspectives toward the problem and possible solutions?

- Has the potential partner worked on the issue in your area? Do they see the gap?

- Do potential member organizations need to address the issue to maintain credibility and influence with the community and decision-makers?

- What would motivate them to participate in the collaborative process, understanding there are competing demands for everyone's attention?

- Have you worked with the organization before? If so, was the relationship productive?

- Do they have special qualities or resources that can add value to the process?

- Do they have financial and human resources they can contribute to the success of the process?

- Does the person who will participate have the skills to co-create boundaries and negotiate the creation of a new structure?

Complementarity

What is *complementarity*? It is when your strengths balance out my weaknesses, when your assets fill in my gaps. Consider whether the potential membership should complement one another when addressing a social mess or complex problem. Wicked issues need a diversity of perspectives to define the problem and discover strategies that work. It is also vital for high-performing work processes; effective groups and problem solving processes value diversity. To look for complementarity, identify those organizations with opposing views, different programming approaches, and different sizes, as well as those that are well-established versus emerging. Keep in mind that the complementary organizations need a common denominator: they are engaged and committed to the issue.

Nils Bohr, the 1922 Nobel Laureate in Physics, is quoted as saying: "The opposite of a correct statement is an incorrect statement. The opposite of a profound truth is another profound truth." Bohr used the word *complementarity* to characterise the relationship between apparently contradictory phenomena. Contradictory phenomenon is a fundamental characteristic of human service delivery systems. Funders want to cut back on funding, yet get more service. They want to pay to the lowest wages but entrust the low paid staff with the most important work, looking after the most vulnerable.

You need to understand all the contradictory approaches and embrace the dilemmas that you face to move forward. Who you invite to the table needs to reflect the contradictions and dilemmas inherent in the system.

People Who Can Act

Getting the right people for the process is often about getting organizational representatives who can act. When I hear about NPOs involved in upwards of over 50 collaboratives, I wonder about the effectiveness of those collaboratives. Is the key decision-maker (usually the executive director) participating in all those collaborations? If not, how is the staff person empowered to act and make decisions on behalf of the originating organization? This is one of the largest obstacles to effective collaboration in the NPO sector. Most people attending meetings of a collaborative are not empowered to act. Their originating organizations have no partnership policy to guide them, therefore they avoid making decisions about participating in or undertaking the work of the collaborative. One way of including people in your process who can act is to ask everyone to develop an in-house collaboration policy. See Chapter 3 for details.

Reflection Questions for a Potential Member

Invitations to participate in collaborative processes sometimes arrive on daily basis. Many NPOs participate in too many processes and feel a high level of burnout by taking on too much. On the other hand, the IASCP report found that most collaboration was only taking place at an informal level. Invitations need to be carefully considered and chosen to further the organization's mission, improve client outcomes, and maximize the use of existing resources.

Potential members should consider the following questions:

- Does the issue affect a large segment of the population you serve?

- Is anyone else working on the issue in your area? Is there a gap?

- Do you need to participate for your group to maintain credibility and influence with the community and decision-makers?

- Does the issue build on your previous successes?

- If you take on the issue, can you find the resources to facilitate your organization's participation?

- Does the issue align with your organizational weaknesses or strengths?

- Do you have a partnership policy that provides guidance and parameters to the organization members who will participate?

- Does your organization's representative to the collaborative have the higher level communication, negotiation, and political skills to be an effective member?

- What power can you contribute to the process and can you harness with other members?

Be sure to identify the criteria that apply to your situation and strategic direction. This should already be spelled out in your organization's collaboration policy, described in Chapter 3.

Key Governance Decision in Step 3

The key governance decision at this stage is to select who gets to play in the sandbox. After you develop the criteria and build a decision framework to guide member selection, decisions that you can justify to broader stakeholders and the community may be obvious. However, sometimes it may be too politically charged for the convener or convening organization to make member selection decisions by themselves. In that case, enlist a convening committee to share the decision-making or hold public consultations to identify possible members. This may be politically risky, as those who oppose changing the status quo may use the consultations to make suggestions contrary to the success of the future collaborative.

The ultimate in shared decision-making is a grassroots semi-electoral representation process, also known as a *snowball process*. A snowball process involves going out into the community and asking people to nominate who they think should participate. Usually the question focus is something like, "Who will represent the best interests of the community/sector at this table?" Once all the suggestions are tabulated, the top 20 or so (or whatever you think appropriate) get to participate in the process.

Collaboratives are consumed with power and turf issues!

It has to be this way. At this stage you will be faced with power and turf issues. Questions about the power base of potential members will constantly cross your mind. If you understand that power is the energy to make things happen, you will want to harness it for your social change work. That some of your potential members have more power than others will be inevitable. Some may have large budgets and staff resources to draw upon, others might be well-connected politically, have specialized expertise or serve a specialized target population, while others may be funders and decision-makers. A collaborative, even when not engaged in political and advocacy work, is an aggregation of the power of its members. The assembly of this power gives the collaborative its unique ability to deal with complex problems, while at the same time providing endless challenges for its members to manage. Power is discussed throughout this book because governance is the structure put in place to deal with power relations.

Collaborative processes assemble knowledge to tackle complex problems. The potential members of a collaborative can be considered as knowledge specialists when invited into the process. They will be expected to participate in the learning and sharing that goes on while exploring the problem set. When it comes time to make decisions, you want people at the table able to make the tough decisions. Finding the right people needs careful consideration, both by those doing the inviting and those doing the accepting.

CHAPTER 8 STEP 4:
Collaborative Planning: Exploring common ground and committing to work together

Vision without action is merely a dream. Action without vision just passes the time. Vision with action can change the world.—Joel A. Barker

At Step 4, you develop the common vision and action strategy. This chapter explores the tools required to overcome differences and competing agendas and to motivate the collaborative membership to work to develop a common strategy. Before learning can take place and decisions are made, the participants need to develop a common language by defining terms and jargon that can cause misunderstanding in communication. Only then can you hope to move diverse organizations and people toward collective action. A participative and inclusive planning process is necessary to build trust and find common ground. Setting the vision and strategic direction is the principal governance function at this step. In simpler terms, you are trying to get a lot of people on a train that is going in one direction. Without their agreement and consent, the train will not leave the station. This step helps create the time and space to have the conversation about why and where the train is going, what is in it for the passengers, and what they will get when the train arrives.

Approving the strategic direction of an organization is a traditional board governance function. In a collaborative, this activity must be assumed by the decision-making body. As the collaborative members are knowledge resources, they bring their knowledge to the process of learning, planning, and assuming the direction-setting governance function. Direction-setting is also known as strategic planning. Whatever you call it, by transforming the disparate knowledge of collaborative members in a collective plan, you discover the key to making system change happen. Some collaboratives may choose to invite others, such as external stakeholders, into the planning process to ensure broader representation. It is wise to include staff, at a minimum the most senior. My preference is to keep the group membership stable to build a highly functional group that will provide leadership during planning and implementation.

Prior to developing a vision and strategy, some groups invest in the development of a mission statement. The vision is what you aspire to, whereas the mission is your purpose. Some advocate developing the mission after the vision, and some before. Many even question the value of a mission statement. I have included further discussion and a tool to develop a mission statement in Chapter 9.

Build a Lexicon (Glossary of Terms) Prior to Collaborative Planning

Once you establish an open and honest climate, the group needs to explore the language issue. In many community-based processes that cross sector and professional boundaries, a single word can mean very different things to different kinds of people (e.g., counsellor vs. probation officer). And when collaborative processes include end users and community members who are unfamiliar with the jargon, the use of technical language quickly alienates them.

Almost all marginalized groups feel they are the victims of professionals who have the power to define their so-called problems and develop expert-based strategies to solve them. Most of these efforts are not successful because they do not take into account the multiple perspectives, sectoral and professional cultures, and regulatory regimes that have jurisdiction or interest in the problem set. They also do not consider the perspectives of the user, client, or survivor. The explicit purpose of a collaborative is to transcend these boundaries of understanding. A collaborative's members need to move toward adapting the same definitions. An emerging collaborative needs to initially develop a shared definition of collaboration. This is critical capacity building, and time must be taken to work through the different understandings.

A lexicon is a glossary of terms that are used in your discussions. To get through the discussions and decision-making involved in building strategies for a complex problem, you need to have a common language. There must also be widespread agreement about the terms and target issues. It is wise to start building this lexicon at the first meeting. It must be created in a climate where there are no stupid questions, and where people can feel comfortable in their lack of clarity.

Start by asking participants to indicate the terms that are new for them or that they may use differently. For instance, in a community health centre, an addiction treatment worker will use the term *intervention* quite differently than a doctor or a community developer will. List the contentious words on a flip chart, along with the agreed upon definition or usage. As this list develops, incorporate it into the terms of reference document and other governance documents. Until the glossary is widely agreed upon, group discussions will be fraught with misunderstandings. Using plain language for definitions will not alienate anyone, and will be more inclusive to all.

Learning about Each Other

A collaborative process builds a learning community. At the first meeting, set the tone to create a climate of tolerance, an appreciation of diversity, and a welcoming atmosphere. Icebreaking exercises to help people get to know one another are a wonderful way to begin the first meeting. It is also wise to have each member share what their organization needs out of the process. A "hopes and fears" icebreaker can help set the tone. For instructions see Chapter 11. By developing an understanding of the different missions of member organizations and the needs of individuals coming on their behalf, the members of the emerging collaborative can be open with their needs and expressions of self-interest. This goes a long way toward building comfort about discussing delicate issues like political dynamics and "who gets what" issues.

Create an Inclusive and High Functioning Group

Will Schutz, a major organization theoretician, proposes a three-stage model of group development: inclusion, control, and affection.

Group members have:

STAGE 1: INCLUSION NEEDS

- Happens early in the group formation process
- Want to interact with others (to get to know who they are dealing with)
- Want to be comfortable in the group and to feel like they belong
- Want to be seen as having a particular identity

STAGE 2: CONTROL NEEDS

- Need for power, influence, and authority
- To ensure their power needs are addressed-their perspectives get heard
- Can run in some people as a desire for control over others—and over one's future. In others by a desire to be controlled—have responsibility lifted

STAGE 3: AFFECTION NEEDS
• Emotional climate is peaceful and tasks are achieved effortlessly
• Close emotional feelings between people
• Phase in which productivity is highest

Schutz's Stage Theory

In the inclusion phase, people encounter each other and decide if they will continue the association. If you do not create a welcoming climate in the first meeting, there may not be a second. Conflict is inevitable. It usually happens after people feel comfortable enough with each to be more themselves—the second stage of group development. Often members with higher control needs have strong opinions that they want the group to adopt and an ensuing struggle to control emerges. Many people, especially those who prefer to avoid conflict or associate strong negative assumptions with it, feel the group is in danger and want to suppress the conflict.

However, keep in mind that conflict is part of the process in a collaborative. You need to have members with control needs to drive the process forward. If no-one cares enough to argue for their perceptions and positions, the energy will not be there to develop a common vision and position for the whole group. Too many members with high control needs can derail the process. Leadership means knowing when to back off from your own need for control.

Once the group gets comfortable with conflict, it can move to the third stage—affection—and build close interpersonal relationships. These relationships hold the collaborative together and create the trust that allows great work to happen. It is important to constantly foster relationship building, even in the third stage, as any changes (such as group members coming and going) cause the group to cycle back to Stage 1. Keep in mind that with every new group member, the group reverts back to the inclusion stage. If the membership is ever-changing, the group dynamics may never move past the inclusion phase. Group development theory and dynamics are further explained in Chapter 12.

Value of a Neutral Facilitator

A facilitator is a trained process expert who leads a meeting through interactive exercises, is neutral (without a stake in the outcome of the meeting), and can move a group through the stages of group development. A facilitator needs to be objective and on an equal level with participants. The facilitator's primary task is to hold the group to its task by creating a climate of acceptance, warmth, and belonging, and to encourage and support the full contribution of each and every member of the group. Facilitators listen more than they speak. In essence, neutral facilitation provides the organization with a natural capability to tap into the hidden potential of all group members, and enables the organization to create a new culture of:

- involvement, that encourages people to participate actively and to think creatively;

- positive management, where people are involved in problem solving and decision-making;

- ownership, where people see themselves as partners and have a strong sense of responsibility and commitment to their organization; and

- integrity, where trust is built and nurtured through an open and caring flow of information.

Individual agendas or political dynamics often intrude violently into the group. The facilitator, while not ignoring such events, needs to ensure that they do not derail the group. If a member of the group facilitates, there is always the risk of that someone will harbour suspicion for the direction the group takes.

At this stage, investing in an outside facilitator who is trained in planning methodologies builds a solid foundation of trust and commitment to the strategy. Saying all that, many groups do not have the funds to hire an external facilitator. Sometimes a trained facilitator is available in a supporting NPO or capacity building organization, such as a volunteer centre, social planning council, or United Way. If not, and if a member of the group is trained in facilitation, you could ask him or her to design and lead the process with strict boundaries in place. These primary boundaries need to be in place to ensure the facilitator takes a neutral position and does not speak on his or her organization's behalf. Someone else should attend the meeting on behalf of the organization.

Secondly, the entire group must agree to this role for the facilitator. If anyone in the group distrusts the proposed facilitator, it needs to be said upfront. Distrust will undermine the facilitation work.

Thirdly, trained facilitators will create an honest and open climate to discuss all the difficult topics like politics, power, and money. They should not be manipulating the agenda and meeting design to achieve prominence for their own or their organization's interests. But this may occur; if you see it, call it and nip it in the bud. It is unethical behaviour for a trained facilitator.

Large Groups Breed Anxiety

When the size of a group gets above about 12 people, unconscious forces can become significant. The need to make Nobel Prize-quality contributions inhibits many people in a large group because they fear that their words will seem silly or inadequate. As a result, the flow of offerings, which are the stuff of good conversation, dries up and there is a sense of "stuckness" and lack of cohesion in the group. Productive change becomes impossible, and the status quo is reinforced by default.

Knowing all that, now what? The governance questions at Step 4 provides a way to build agreement on what the plan should be. For example:

• How do you tackle the task of developing a common vision and action plan when you have diverse viewpoints at the table?

• How will you synthesize all the knowledge embodied in these human representatives?

• How will you provide a time and space for all participants to learn from each other?

At the same time, you (or preferably a neutral facilitator) need to take the budding collaborative through the stages of group development. This will help members feel comfortable (inclusion stage) enough to put their interests out on the table, stand up for what they believe in (control stage), build enough trust to begin to agree (affection stage), and start to work on the task of developing a common vision and strategy to address the complex problem. The group is in learning mode as it moves through these stages.

Type of Change

To address long-standing complex social issues, whole systems must change. A whole system includes all the stakeholders' organizations and individuals who are integral to the functioning of that system. Sometimes the players are not aware that they are indeed part of the system. For example, NPOs often do not see themselves as part of a government system, as parents do not see themselves as part of the education system. Change requires stakeholder self-acknowledgement, which why member selection is so critical.

When you are engaged in member selection, you are mapping the system and discovering the connections that sustain the system. Many of the diverse stakeholders are not aware of their relationships, or do not have sufficiently developed relationships to work together to address common issues. Traditionally, decision-makers would rather invest in expert-led processes that diagnose and propose solutions in written reports. Academic and professional systems support this narrow problem solving approach, and at times it may suffice.

> As such, project approaches to change bring their own inbuilt or implicit theory of social change to the development sector, premised on an orientation of simple cause and effect thinking. It goes something like this: In a situation that needs changing we can gather enough data about a community and its problems, analyze it and discover an underlying set of related problems and their cause, decide which problems are the most important, redefine these as needs, devise a set of solutions and purposes or outcomes, plan a series of logically connected activities for addressing the needs and achieving the desired future results, as defined up front, cost the activities into a convincing budget, raise the funding and then implement the activities, monitor progress as we work to keep them on track, hopefully achieve the planned results and at the end evaluate the project for accountability, impact and sometimes even for learning. (Reeler, article undated, p. 5)

As Reeler's quote so aptly describes, in efforts to professionalize the sector you should seek evaluative evidence for programming decisions. In trying to justify everything, you still cannot tame the complexity with rational approaches. Rational approaches, which include adopting more business-like behaviour—better management, focused prioritization, and evaluation tools—may result in a clear business plan and better run programs, but the complexity of dealing with wicked human and social problems undermines any forecast you can come up with.

Instead, a non-linear approach may be necessary when the problems are complex and there is inherent conflict in the stagnant system. You need to move away from the belief that simple changes to the system will fix what is broken. Complex issues require the mobilizing of a broad range of system actors as issue owners and decision-makers in the change process.

It is time-consuming to map the system, identify appropriate collaborative members, and then coordinate an event to bring them all together and create mutual awareness. However, this is the only way to achieve the higher orders of change identified in Table 5.

Table 5: Criteria for Distinguishing Orders of Change in Problem Solving Initiatives

CRITERIA	FIRST ORDER CHANGE	SECOND ORDER CHANGE	THIRD ORDER CHANGE
DESIRED OUTCOME	"More (or less) of the same."	Reform	Transformation
PURPOSE	To improve the performance of the established system.	To change the system to address shortcomings and respond to the needs of stakeholders	To address problems from a whole system perspective
CRITERIA	FIRST ORDER CHANGE	SECOND ORDER CHANGE	THIRD ORDER CHANGE
PARTICIPATION	To replicate the established decision-making group and power relationships.	To bring relevant stakeholders into the problem solving conversation in ways that enable them to influence the decision-making process.	To create a microcosm of the problem system, with all participants coming in on an equal footing as issue owners and decision-makers.
PROCESS	To confirm existing rules. Preserves the established power structure and relationships among actors in the system.	To open existing rules to revision. Suspends established power relationships; promotes authentic interactions; creates a space for genuine reform of the system.	To open the issue to creation of entirely new ways of thinking about the issue. Promotes transformation of relationships toward whole-system awareness and identity; promotes examination of the deep structures that sustain the system; creates a space for fundamental system change.

Adapted from Waddell, Steve Social Integration: A Global Societal Learning and Change Perspective, A Presentation to the United Nations Department of Economic and Social Affairs Expert Group Meeting on Dialogue in the Social Integration Process. New York2005. Downloaded from http://www.instituteforstrategicclarity.org/Publications/SocialIntegrationSteveWaddell.doc.

Table 5 lines up nicely with Zimmerman's typology of problems that was presented in Chapter 5. Third order change is needed when your problems are complex or wicked.

Where are you now?

You know that you need transformative change to tackle a complex problem set. In Step 3, you brought together the knowledge resources and wisely hired a consultant to help the collaborative group come together to develop a vision and strategy to address the problem set. As in any good problem solving process, you need to define and explore the problem or problem set. In the complex problem/ large system scenario, it is vital that everyone builds this understanding together face-to-face. As the convener, you may have spent time doing this in Step 1. You may have been very thorough, but still everything you have learned so far is just a piece of the problem puzzle. You need the other members of the collaborative to build the common language used to understand the problem. The multiple perspectives will help identify all the causal factors and define the problem so that everyone understands. In this way, participants understand perspectives other than their own and learn how various factors interplay. The result is a unique complexity associated with the subject. Understanding why the system acts the way it does opens up the possibility for change.

Many new theories are now available to undertake this task. Complex adaptive theory, systems theory, and game theory are three approaches that look to scope out the terrain of complex problems and provide tools to identify the patterns. Many people are overwhelmed at this step and continue to rely on experts or technology to analyze the problem set, rather than bringing all the knowledge resources to the table. After all, people are the most complex systems of all, and totally unpredictable most of the time. It is no wonder that decision-makers choose the predictability of outside expertise or technology to define a problem, rather than invest in a labour-intensive process of collaborative learning. Experts may have a highly developed perspective of the problem, but if the system players are not involved in the learning/change process they have no impetus to change.

While many technical investments are fine for sharing and distributing information, few effectively transform information into wisdom and provide a satisfactory learning environment where there is exploration and negotiation amongst various perspectives. There is a real push by many funders and early technology adopters to have people communicate and work in a cyber environment. But for intensive learning to occur, a real-time, interactive, face– to-face process is necessary. At this stage, the group process need to honour self-interest and encourage open discussion amongst the process actors who have inherent conflict with each other. So far, nothing has convinced me otherwise. Online collaboration is better left to resolve day-to-day matters and share information when a relationship has been built. Communication experts say that 70% of our communication is non-verbal. In my view, you need that non-verbal communication to satisfy others that what you say or state in writing is congruent with your body language.

Self-interest tinges all the perspectives around the table. For instance, if you run a shelter, when you address the complex problem of homelessness you may advocate for more housing. You might also say this because if the collaborative can establish the need for more shelter beds, then maybe your organization will be the recipient of more funds. Another member might provide food programming and know the value of filling up people's stomachs, and want a piece of the funding pie to go to increased food security. Neither perspective is wrong, and both are completely valid. Both act in their respective organization's self-interest, and unless they play the game, they may later find that the other organization gets the bulk of any new resources or new territory. Other stakeholders around the table will not accommodate your needs if you do not put them out there. A skilled facilitator can make the space safe enough for participants to be open and honest so that the conversation will flow as easily as at a great dinner party.

Where do you want to be?

After exploring the problem and there is a collective sigh of relief that nothing is left hidden or unsaid, the task becomes taking all that learning and knowledge and transcending differences to find common ground. Common ground is located in the words of a collective vision and the goals of an action plan. A vision is more than a strategic plan for how to address an issue. A vision is a picture of the desired future and what you ultimately hope to accomplish as a result of your efforts. The action of creating a vision forces you to take a stand for a preferred future. The vision takes over from self-interest and appeals to your higher selves and ideals.

To forge a common vision, the collaborative needs to have the whole system in the room, that is, the same people who explored the problem. By building knowledge with and about the whole system, participants can make better decisions that incorporate not only their area of expertise, but that build an understanding of how all the parts influence the whole. The vision is also a way of discovering that serving the collaborative serves your organization's self-interest. Your vision channels your deepest values and becomes a word picture of what you want your values to be, lived out in your alliance coalition or partnership.

Not just any vision will do. Because you choose to pursue your vision in the uncharted territory between government and sole autonomous organizations, it needs to be both strategic and lofty. The strategic element of a vision involves staying focused on your end target group or service users to express how you will achieve the mission or purpose of the collaborative. This helps connect each goal and objective with something important, namely the success of the vision.

A vision is very different from goals and objectives. Goals and objectives are basically a prediction of what is to come. A vision is the preferred future, a desirable and ideal state, whereas the mission is the group's purpose (e.g., our group works to reduce poverty). Your vision will likely include your mission, but it will change over time to adapt to changing conditions, while your mission will likely remain constant. The vision of a collaborative defines who and what the collaborative is about, why it exists, and where it is going in the grand scheme of things. A vision consists of three characteristics:

1. an organization's fundamental reason for existence beyond just making money or providing more service;

2. a description of the timeless unchanging core values of the organization; and

3. a "big picture" aspiration for its own future.

Here are examples of components of vision statements:

- Respect and build on each other's strengths
- Consistency between plans and actions
- A willingness to share
- Disagree without fear
- Celebrate diversity
- Commitment to a long-term strategy
- Live our values
- Treat each person in a unique way
- Overcome hierarchy and rank to create a democratic organization
- A positive attitude, less energy on bad situations
- See caring and love in all actions
- Every person is a leader
- Work as a high performing team
- Each person feels valued and respected
- Provide meaningful work
- Each person and organization has the right to say no
- Control of our own destiny
- Freedom to fail
- Honesty at all times
- Empathy for others' pain
- Each person is heard and understood
- Positive social change
- An oppression-free organization culture
- As strong as our weakest link

Adapted from Block, 1989, p. 111–114.

As Peter Block, an organizational thought leader, says, "If your vision statement sounds like motherhood and apple pie and you are somewhat embarrassed, you are on the right track."

Wonderful side effects emerge once you have a comprehensive vision that collaborative members own and are committed to implementing. External decision-makers in other community organizations can start to make decisions moving their resources forward to the desired future. The vision and strategy can also provide a blueprint to funders on the communities' priorities. The vision has political clout; it tells decision-makers and politicians that members of the collaborative have reached consensus on how to handle the problem set. This can provide immense relief to those in office and civil servants because they do not have to forge agreement amongst a community or a sector.

Why doesn't everybody have a vision?
People often feel that the time spent in preparation for action—primarily planning—is a waste of time and feels slow. There is a heightened sense of urgency in the non-profit sector because of the nature of the work. We help people in crisis, and crisis situations call for speedy reactions. However, some crises have lasted for decades, and yet we still bring this tendency to want fast action to collaborative tables when working on highly complex issues. Nothing sabotages a collaborative more than letting this desire for urgency overtake the process. This sense of urgency is fueled by individual anxiety that rapidly infects the membership of a collaborative and shuts down legitimate debate, especially impeding discussion of hot topics. (Some situations are legitimate crisis situations and when they are, there is a suggested process to follow, as discussed in Chapter 11.)

In reality, preparation like visioning and planning enable fast activity during the execution phase. Planning and thoughtful preparation reduce the time and energy lost in figuring out things through trial and error, and bring role and task clarity to all the members and staff involved in executing projects and programs. The military addresses this tendency to move into action with a slogan, "go slow to go fast."

A shared vision is critical for the success of a collaborative. As different organizations with different missions and visions come together, a shared purpose and shared vision is necessary to unite the group and focus it on the complicated and collaborative strategies needed to address complex problems. A collective vision can also address how the group wants to interact with each other. If the group wants to address inherent imbalances, they can be incorporated into the vision with a statement of values or procedures, such as annual community consultations.

How do you get there?

This step answers the question of how you get there: by developing a strategy for building out the collective vision. To bring the vision to life, the group needs to decide what goals and objectives will make the plan a reality. Those goals and objectives need to be measureable so they can be linked to outcomes and results. So, if a new program is needed, the group should develop an action plan as part of this process to guide implementation. Setting up a new program can be the goal, and the objectives are the milestones of the action plan of doing a needs assessment (market research), writing a grant proposal, hiring staff, etc. Goals and objectives are basically predictions of what is to come. They need to follow the development of the vision.

Don't forget: Goals and objectives are also necessary for communication strategies or behaviour change goals.

What's really happening?

By bringing the system actors together, you are initiating a dialogue. We call these *dialogic* approaches because they involve people coming together, seeking to make positive change through conversation and agreement. But there is another process going on, dealing with the *will* to change. Building the will to change amongst system players is done through feeling safe, getting one's needs met, understanding the need for change, and participating in drafting the strategies for change.

You may have heard the term *learning organization*. In effect, a temporary learning organization is constructed to explore the multiple perspectives and knowledge that people bring to the table. Along with learning, negotiations are underway. Transformative change processes are characterized not only by learning, but by unlearning. You need to unlearn the assumptions you hold that keep the system stuck.

For example, a participant in one of my workshops shared her approach when attending a collaborative planning session. Conscious that she will need to engage and negotiate, she uses a framework called *Give, Get, Guard*. Prior to attending the planning event, she thinks about what she is willing to give to the collaborative (such as resources or a staffing or time commitment), what she wants to get out of the process (such as funding or an advocacy objective), and what she will guard (such as her organization's exposure to risk or a bad reputation). This is a great tool to help you plan your strategy when attending a planning event.

Conversation Methodologies

Trained facilitators use many methodologies to help groups move through this step and engage in productive dialogue. These tools include: appreciative inquiry; open space; search conference; and facilitation tools used by the Institute of Cultural Affairs. Most collaboratives with over 10 members engage a facilitator to use a large group method.

All of these tools help to create a safe space to move a group through the stages of inclusion and control, and build in opportunities for dialogue (see Figure 11) to discover common ground. Moving through the entire process requires at least two days of planning work as a group. If the group will not provide the time, the facilitator and the methodology will not have the time required to move the group through the control phase and come to an agreement about the desired future.

Figure 11: Forms of Discourse

Figure 11 shows that there are five different ways of engaging in discourse or conversation. Argument and debate are the two forms commonly associated with conflict and unproductive forms of communication. They often precede violence. While both have their place in communicating anger or when in competition, they are not conducive to building relationships. Inquiry and advocacy are less intense forms of conversation and are very useful in professional settings. One inquires and the other advocates, and the back and forth activity can result in information sharing and negotiation. These are both useful in resolving conflict.

Dialogue is a form of communication in which the goals are understanding and respect. It is different from other forms of communication in several ways. In dialogue, you:

- present your own perspective while listening carefully to the perspectives of others
- remain open to change
- speak for yourself and from personal experience
- allow others to express their perspectives safely
- learn significant new things about yourself and others
- find shared concerns with people who hold different perspectives
- explore doubts and uncertainties
- ask questions out of true curiosity
- explore the complexity of issues without polarization
- collaborate to create better futures.

Guidelines for Dialogue
There are a number of guidelines to follow when conducting a dialogue, including:

- Think of and treat each other as partners and colleagues.

- Suspend assumptions and certainties—hang them out in front of you so that they can be observed and questioned.

- Observe how other comments stir your thinking.

- Don't say what you already know—discover your response as you speak it.

- Observe your thinking.

- Respond to the question, not to the comments of others.

- Stay in inquiry (focus on learning) and out of advocacy (focus on convincing).

The most important governance issue at this step is who has the power to construct the vision and who needs to own it. Much of what is addressed above is building agreement amongst the people at the table. But external to the immediate members of the collaborative are others who have a stake in the vision and eventual outcomes of the interventions. This issue is an extension of the governance issues explored in Step 3, related to who gets to join the collaborative. Closest to the collaborative members is the issue needing the approval of their home organizations. All members need to ask if the vision needs the approval of their home organizations and board of directors. Ask them to check their home organization's collaborative policy. If they do not have one, check with the organization's management on how to proceed.

Further to the internal approval process is the external one. The collaborative may be representative of the problem domain and existing system, but devote some time to determining whether there are others who should have the vision document and be given an opportunity to comment or provide feedback. Public meetings are one way to do this, and distributing the vision document to a broad contact list is another way. Technologically savvy processes include audio conferences and webinars. Using communication technology to communicate is especially time saving when you need buy-in or clear approval from many parties.

Figure 12 illustrates the likely parties and stakeholders who may need input or who might even have the right to ratify a strategic plan developed by a collaborative. First and foremost, include all the collaborative members who participated in the development of the strategy. Members may need to take the plan to their home organization's senior management and their board of directors to adopt a formal motion of approval. If the strategy needs broader support and buy-in, include stakeholders such as other agencies and community organizations who need to be informed of the plan and also endorse or at the very least agree not to oppose it.

Figure 12: Approval Loop

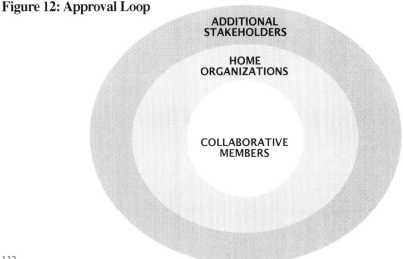

Determining the Collaborative Value Proposition

A value proposition is a term widely-used in the private sector to begin the deal-making process between two or more organizations. Basically, it describes how the organizations are going to make money together, or in other words, glean value from working together. A value proposition can be applied to any for-profit endeavour because in this sector, everything is focused on generating money or profits; the purpose of a firm is to make money.

Since those in government or the NPO sector do not have to make money or profits (although we protect it and make sure it is wisely spent), we sometimes neglect to generate and assess value to the time we invest. It is much harder to determine value when it cannot be expressed in monetary terms. However, there is a monetary investment in collaboratively run projects. Consider the number of hours that you or other staff work on behalf of the collaborative. Hours taken up in meetings and reading and responding to emails are just the beginning of your agency's costs. Once joint projects and committee work are also factored in, some staff members can contribute up to half of their work time to the collaborative. You can then quantify this investment as half of the staffing costs to your agency for this worker.

For example, think of the investment as $30,000, assuming the full-time cost of a worker is approximately $60,000 including benefits (some colleagues in Canada will accuse me of being too generous in this example). However, your collaborative endeavours need to generate value for collaboration members (and their clients), and that value needs to be greater than just using your organizational resources to provide service in the usual manner.

Members of the collaborative need to have positive return on their investment that is equal to the sum of the return on investments for each member of the collaboration, plus the ROI in the collaboration itself.

You might be able to quantify the impact of the collaborative project by the increase in the number of clients served. For instance, consider a half-time worker who services 15 clients per year at an agency. By engaging in a collaborative project, that worker still serves 15 clients at the home agency, plus the agency expects a substantial increase in clients as the result of the collaboration and the pooling of resources. If no new clients are served through a collaboration of three agencies (15 existing clients per agency, the same number of clients as served before the collaboration), then the investment of staffing time generated no return and the collaboration was not worthwhile. Instead, if an additional 15 clients are served, bringing an additional five clients to each agency for a total of 60 clients for all three agencies combined, then there is positive return on the investment of staff time.

With a return on the investment of five new clients for agency A using the same half-time worker, the agency reaped a benefit through the increase in clients served. The same $15,000 that served 15 clients before is now serving 20, representing an increase in productivity of 25%. However, if all those new clients (15) were served by only one of the agencies, say agency A, then there would be no return on the investment of agency B and C.

If the project focus is broader than direct service delivery or a campaign, it is much harder to quantify the impact of joint pooling of resources. But the most important point is that you need to quantify your investment so results can be measured. Start by quantifying the investment of staff time. Even if you are dealing with complex outcomes like community revitalization, you can quantify the time spent in meetings and project work and try to quantify the anticipated outcomes as much as possible. Some anticipated outcomes for a community revitalization collaborative might be increased sales for downtown businesses or an increase in employment, or you might qualitatively measure changes in attitude of key community actors or stakeholders. The key message is that investing in collaboration takes time and money and should be expected to generate positive outcomes. Do not invest your time and energy without thinking hard about the costs and benefits.

Step 4 is all about the process of learning and planning. To support these two processes, you must create the conditions for mutual learning to take place. First, get everyone on the same page in terms of language and develop a glossary of terms. Respect the process of building an inclusive and safe group where conflict and multiple perspectives are normalized. Lastly, build awareness and will to change through conversation. Dialogue facilitated by a neutral facilitator is the best way to answer the questions of where you have been, where you are going, and how you are going to get there. And do not forget to ensure that the collaborative is a good deal for its members. Collaboration is costly and must provide a good return on investments of time, energy, and financial resources.

CHAPTER 9 STEP 5:
Building an organization—
A mechanism to implement the plan

The sun, with all those planets revolving around and dependant on it, can still ripen a bunch of grapes as if it had nothing else in the universe to do.—Galileo

At Step 5, the process becomes an organization—the plan you developed in Step 4 comes to life. It is the most intensive step, requiring resources and usually staffing. The day-to-day building of the group's architecture can lead to opportunity for disagreement and conflict. Power and authority issues may emerge on a daily basis, so conflict needs to be channeled into productive decision making. This chapter looks at how to create a governance framework that recognizes and aggregates the power of the group, including how to produce a mission or charter, and how to design a policy framework with enough organizational policies to support the day-to-day work of organization building. The governance framework also includes designing an organizational structure, which was discussed in chapter 4.

New collaboratives can be temporary, short-lived organizations, or they may be around for years to come. No matter what the timeframe, the created structure needs to support implementation of the strategy or intervention. As the work progresses, hundreds of decisions will need to be made. Who will make what kinds of decisions is in essence the governance structure. Although a common belief is that boards are only responsible for governance, in the NPO sector the work of governance in collaboratives is often undertaken by staff from the member organizations. These staff people may never have been exposed to their home organization's governance activities and bodies (board and committees). However, now they find themselves participating in the day-to-day or governance work of a collaborative and unknowingly taking on a governance role. In their home organizations they are the implementers, but in the collaborative they are the governing decision-makers—and most likely doing a lot of the everyday work as well.

In an organization, a board of directors holds legal liability for any funding received and holds fiduciary responsibility for monies spent. In a collaborative—unless there is a designated lead agency or trustee assigned with the legal and financial responsibility of accountability and oversight—every organization's board of directors that belongs to the collaborative holds joint legal responsibility for the actions of the collaborative. Whoever signs the documents accepting funding or any form of legal document is the body with fiscal and legal responsibility. Governance refers to the collaborative's processes and procedures that ensure proper functioning, resolve conflict, and make the job of oversight easier for the body assigned with legal accountability (i.e., a trustee, fiscal sponsor, or member's board of directors). Home organizations also have to be careful and monitor the collaboratives they belong to and ensure proper oversight over monies and human resources.

At this step, the group develops the organizational infrastructure needed to implement the common vision and plan. The task is to organize the vision and action into structure, leadership, communication, policies, and procedures to support strategy implementation and streamline the ongoing work and decision-making. Not all the work at this step is governance, but this is the most governance-intensive step, with the creation of a structure and assumption of ongoing work functions.

Many collaboratives are stymied by this phase, wanting to move forward to make the plan happen, while ignoring the need to build organizational capacity. A collaborative is often built without members ever considering what they need to do to survive and thrive as a semi-autonomous organization. Instead, members bravely continue until conflict or lack of participation grabs everyone's attention or simply kills off the process. To help stave off the tendency of high failure rates for collaboratives in this phase, I presented a tri-process model of trans-organizational effectiveness in my first book. The model includes trust-building processes, governance processes, and work coordination processes. This model emphasizes the construction of the governance processes without losing sight of the need to build trust and coordinate/manage the work. Both streams of work are vital to ensure that the plan is successfully operationalized. Your collaborative may have an established governance framework, but if there is little trust amongst the members, more than likely they will not engage in conflict resolution and just walk away.

The same holds true for work coordination. The work of a collaborative is complex. It requires that support staff have the political skills to work with diverse organizational cultures, as well as great interpersonal skills to manage the needs of all the partners, and program and management skills to run an autonomous NPO. Governance is only one aspect of collaborative development, albeit an important one. See the chapter on leadership for a more in-depth discussion on the skills needed to lead and to support a collaborative.

The Collaborative's Authority to Govern
The collaborative's authority and power to act is derived from its empowerment and consolidation of power by its members' organizations. If it is incorporated or trusteed by an incorporated body, then its authority to operate is derived from its incorporation under federal provincial or state law and its constitution and bylaws. If it is incorporated, then it must have a board of directors and be first and foremost accountable to that board (which is likely why few collaboratives choose to incorporate). Member control and influence has to be subjugated to its board of directors, and the organizational structure replicates a regular non-profit.

Most NPOs belong to membership organizations such as sector organizations. A traditional industry association is almost always incorporated and is governed by a board of directors coming from the ranks of the membership organizations. When there are hundreds of member organizations, a member organization is unlikely to have a representative on the board. The amount of control over the actions of the membership organization is minimal, and if the industry association is aligned with the desires and interests of their members, there is likely not a problem with this. Broader involvement of the membership can come through sub-committees and conferences.

This form of representative organization is especially valuable in policy and government relations work. The membership organization builds a consensus amongst its members and presents a united position to a government on issues relevant to its membership. The power relationships are clear and governments are comfortable with this structure. These days, industry associations spend much time at government consultations because they are clearly the voice of an industry or sector. All of this clarity comes with a price: the construction of internal organizational capacity to provide services to its members and provide opportunities to develop strategy.

The permutations of issue ownership and relevance do not always align with traditional sector organizations. In Canada, sector organizations are often organized along provincial (state) boundaries and for one particular funding stream (e.g., immigration and settlement). Yet many NPO political issues are emerging at the regional and municipal level and are pertinent to NPOs funded by many different funders. To fill in the gaps in urgent situations, NPOs turn to collaboratives to consolidate their power into a unified voice, while building only as much infrastructure as necessary. This process of wanting to act quickly, of not building a new organization, and of consolidating power and resources to stay involved in decision-making are all motivations to invest power and resources into a collaborative form of organization, rather than build a new NPO. Additional authority to act comes from the organization's mission, as well as any rights and responsibilities that come from the expectations outlined in funding or fee-for-service agreements.

After what is legally required under law and funding agreements, the collaborative governance structure is a product of the negotiations between its members and possibly its stakeholders.

Why should you care about putting a governance structure in place?
Governance defines the division of power within an organization and establishes mechanisms to achieve accountability between members, stakeholders, its governing body, and management. Decisions about governance create organizational capacity. When organizational capacity is agreed to, then commitment to the plan and its implementation is enhanced. If members fear the building of organizational capacity and if people do not continue to come together and interact, there likely will be little in the way of collective implementation activity. A governance structure ensures there are mechanisms to get the work done, roles and responsibilities, and leadership and accountability. Most importantly, a governance structure provides a mechanism for conflict resolution to resolve differences throughout the implementation process. You can construct decision-making and planning processes to address any inherent power imbalances. If you move ahead and pretend that there is equal power sharing or that the community has a voice, you will only pay later with more intense conflict. Governance conversations help members understand their rights and responsibilities to the collaborative.

The most common group dynamic in a collaborative is the avoidance dynamic. You see this in meetings of long-standing collaboratives, where the meeting basically consists of a round-robin process. Members report on their organization's latest program initiative, and someone might share a bit of intelligence or relay a concern. After all the reports are done, there might be a bit of discussion around the latest concerns, perhaps leading to agreement on an action to take. However, since most members are unaware of their roles and responsibilities and have not been empowered by their home organization to participate, they do not participate. All the possibilities for great work though collaboration do not materialize.

Governance structures support and normalize conflict, especially for those who are uncomfortable with it. Accept that there will be conflict and make provisions for it. Then, when there is conflict that needs to be dealt with, the process will be in place and conflict will be normalized. A governance structure provides information about your organization and a level of comfort to funders. It tells them that you know enough to build the capacity for open decision-making and appropriate power-sharing.

All the following governance issues deal with power and competing interests:

• need for a clear mission and vision
• meeting management
• decision-making
• inter-organizational turf issues
• power differentials between people and organizations
• organization structure
• need for trust building
• forced or incented collaboration

Governance structures provide a way to avoid getting mired in conflict, or to avoid the conflict that needs to be addressed to achieve enough agreement to move the collaborative forward in its work. A collaborative organizational structure allows for flexibility. You need to ensure enough governance is in place to support the work, but with enough flexibility to make system changes.

Who governs in a collaborative?

It is critical that collaboratives are empowered to make decisions on an ongoing basis, are entrusted with managing resources, and are accountable to funders, member organizations, and the community. If the decisions are made by only one organization or a government, it is not a collaborative; however, this may be perfectly acceptable for a policy consultation process or a network. Although governance is not needed in these situations, it still has a great deal of value;

however, in this case the convening institution has the power and is not sharing that power with others. In the case of a government, it is generally legally restricted from doing so. Participation in these policy consultations means you are only providing input and advice, not sharing in decision-making.

Governance directs decision-making and vice versa, usually by a steering committee comprised of representatives from all the member organizations. If the collaborative chooses not to incorporate, then there is no legal responsibility for a board of directors. If the collaborative does not receive funding it is not an issue. However, this becomes problematic from an accountability standpoint if the receipt and management of funding is involved. The critical governance decision point comes when the collaborative has to decide whether it wants to create a new autonomous governance structure or adopt the framework of one of its members or another incorporated body who will act as a trustee.

Established agencies are often called upon to act as a trustee to enable an emerging collaborative to qualify for funding opportunities. Sometimes one of the members of a collaborative fulfils this function, or some foundations also do this as service. For instance, the Tides Canada Initiatives (TCI) Foundation acts as a trustee for many environmental collaboratives. However, TCI is not a trustee as most of us understand it, but rather it is a separate charitable entity set up as a fiscal sponsor.[13] As with any collaborative process, responsibilities and roles need to be negotiated between the trustee/sponsor and the collaborative decision-making body.

How do you create a governance structure for a collaborative?
At the point when you involve another organization, you begin to develop the governance structure. The first governance question to address is who makes what decision, and how are you going to organize the two (or more of you) to do so. Will you make decisions in meetings? Will you have meetings on a regular basis? No matter what structural arrangements you adopt, the functions of governance must be undertaken and implemented. If you have not yet formalized your decision-making process and meeting details, then use the following tool prior to developing the common vision and strategic directions discussed in Chapter 8. Collaboratives can develop both a terms of reference and a mission statement. If you are in Step 3, are having meetings, and are not yet moving into Step 4 (the collaborative planning phase), these next two tools will build enough internal capacity to hold meetings and recruit members.

[13] For more information got to http://tidescanada.org/focus/strengthening-charities-non-profits/

Terms of Reference

When there is more than one partner and the problem scoping and planning steps are going to take some time, it is best to establish a temporary structure to support decision-making and meetings until after the vision is established and more is known about the intervention. You can use a terms of reference or process charter, the simplest form of organization, to accomplish this task (sometimes also called a covenant). In effect, this document is a process contract for the collaborative members. It is most useful at the early stages of collaborative development. Later on, you can transform the content of your terms of reference into a collaborative agreement, which has more legal weight.

A terms of reference document must include the following:

- name of the group

- when and how often you meet

- definition of a quorum (the number of members who must be there to do official business and make decisions—usually at least half)

- who facilitates the meeting and who takes minutes

- whether you will use Roberts Rules of Order (i.e., parliamentary procedure) or consensus decision-making (or a modified version of either)

- funding expectations (or lack thereof)—what people pay, when and how they pay it

Mission Statement:

A mission statement sums up your collaborative's reason for being. It answers the question, what is our purpose for coming together? It explains your intentions, priorities, and values to people both inside and outside the group. It can guide you and help you stay focused on the things that are most important. If you ever question whether to take on a project or choose a particular course of action, look back on your mission statement and see if the proposal is consistent with it.

Developing a Mission Statement

Use the answers to the following questions as a guide for drafting a mission statement for your collaborative.

1) What do you hope to accomplish as a result of your efforts?

2) How do you plan to accomplish these goals?

3) For whose benefit does your organization exist?

Weave together your responses from these questions into a single statement.

The mission of our organization is:

_____

_____

_____

In the IT world, project managers use a project charter to define the project objectives and the authority of the project manager, clarify roles and responsibilities of project members, and identify reporting lines for decision-making and accountability. A project charter is synonymous with a mission statement and terms of reference.

Bylaws

The development of bylaws is usually associated with the legal incorporation process. In practice, bylaws can be brief or lengthy. To ensure that there is adequate organizational structure, at a minimum incorporation acts usually identify the required number of directors, the decision-making process (i.e., voting procedure: majority rules as consensus is not permitted), and some meeting management rules. If you want to incorporate, you need to see a lawyer, or you can use do-it-yourself kits designed to meet local legislation for your province or state that are available on the Web.[14]

However, if you adopt a trustee to funnel through your funding, you automatically have to comply with its incorporation and by-laws. That does not mean your collaborative cannot adopt a consensus decision-making procedure, it just means that when the trustee board of directors passes your proposal for funding or report to funder, it must use its voting procedure to pass its motion and approve your document. There are areas where it is critical to comply with trustee policy, and I will explore them later.

If there are minimalist bylaws or a trustee, the rest of the rules of governance need to be fleshed out in a policy framework. With incorporation, it is more desirable to have decisions spelled out in a policy framework because the steering committee

---

[14] In Ontario, Canada, the Ministry of the Attorney General provides a free resource: the Not-for-Profit
Incorporator's Handbook. Available at http://www.attorneygeneral.jus.gov.on.ca/english/family/pgt/nfpinc/.

can then change them in a regular meeting. If they are included in the bylaws (depending on local laws), you may need to hold a general members' meeting to change them, which is a lot of work when you want to include a new member or change a rule. Instead, policies should spell out who can be members, their roles and responsibilities, how to manage finances, and governing human resources and communication guidelines. To help in your roles and responsibilities planning, the RASCI tool is provided in appendix F. The RASCI model assigns responsibility when planning a project to ensure the assignments are carried out.

A Cautionary Note about Shared Responsibilities
Governance is all about responsibility. In the governance role, you are a steward of other people's money and resources with a public trust to spend it to meet a social need. This is really a leadership role where you put your own needs aside and look at creating social good in the world. Governance policies and processes will not prevent determined people from defrauding the public or community's purse. In a way, governance is a tool for control and oversight to contain the potential opportunist who may see resources as a means for personal gain.

Ideally,

- the leadership of the collaborative governs the organization through its policy and priority-setting role;

- the executive director or most senior staff person manages the programs and services;

- if there are staff, they implement the programs and services.

However, collaborative steering committees are often like developing boards of NPOs where they need to keep a hands-on approach, as long as they also attend to strategic matters. A steering committee should not only attend to strategic matters; a hands-on approach is often effective. If the collaborative does not have staff, then there is no one else to do the work and members must step in until additional resources arrive. In many cases a staff person manages meetings, but staff members are not available to implement the strategy.

From Saidel (1998), Bradshaw (2000), and others' perspectives, there is no one ideal governance model but there are certain governance functions which must be fulfilled by the nonprofit. According to them it does not matter who performs the governance functions as long as the functions are being performed. (Bradshaw, 2002)

Governance Models

Leaders in NPO circles currently are paying a lot of attention to governance models. Models are particular approaches to governance that are defined by the following attributes: a set of structures, functions, and practices that define who does what and how they do it. These attributes typically relate to the role and relationships of the board of directors and the senior staff member of an organization (CEO or executive director).

Structure: defined by incorporation, constitutions, and bylaws or prescribed directly by legislation.

Functions: refers to the roles of different players involved in governance.

Practices: refers to how governance activities such as policy-making are approached.

There are typically three types of NPO governance models:

• policy governance board (associated with John Carver)

• working/administrative board

• collective

A model for collaborative governance is often more like a working administrative board, similar to a new non-profit organization where there are few staff members and those who govern are also volunteers who do much of the organizational work. When a collaborative chooses a democratic and power sharing form of organizational structure, it will develop more of a collective model of governance where each member has one vote and participates in most decision-making. The workload depends on the funding available to hire staff or available volunteer resources.

Needless to say, many organizational leaders resist spending valuable time in routine decision-making and want to only participate in direction setting or financial decision-making. They may have experience with policy governance and wish to have the collaborative governing body move toward more of a policy-making role. It is a matter of what is needed at the time, and what staffing resources are available to allow the collaborative governors to take more of a hands-off role. Policy governance requires a lot of staff support and a hands-off attitude by those who govern. But governing with policy does not have to be as hands-off as prescribed in Carver's policy governance model. When moving toward creating policy to streamline direct decision-making, it is wise to keep in mind that you want a flexible and supportive governance framework for changing conditions.

The term *function* refers to the roles of different players involved in governance. These three functions are basically what a board of directors would do for a NPO. However, in a collaborative the community representation broadens to include organization representation and is undertaken by the body that is making decisions for the collaborative.

As shown in Figure 13, the three primary governance functions are:

• community and organizational representation

• leadership through policy and decision-making

• monitoring and evaluation

Figure 13: Three Primary Governance Functions

MONITORING AND
EVALUATION

COMMUNITY AND
ORGANIZATIONAL
REPRESENTATION

LEADERSHIP
THROUGH POLICY
AND DECISION
MAKING

The Community Representation Function
The dynamics of representing the community pose a greater challenge in matters of accountability. Appropriate accountability must ultimately focus on the community level because the collaborative is composed of publicly funded or regulated organizations now entrusted with a mandate to deal with a complex social problem. At the same time, you must create accountability systems to keep

the collaborative accountable to the member organizations who are contributing resources to the process, and have boards of directors accountable for the fiscal and human resources invested in the collaborative. It is vital for organizational representatives to voice their needs to accommodate their organization's internal management and decision structures. The member organizations' boards of directors are also responsible for representing the community at the organization's table. A linkage or direct channel needs to be made between the community as a stakeholder or owner of the member agency and the agency's interests and perspectives at the collaborative table.

On a practical level, the act of representing the community in a governance context involves asking questions such as:

- What does your community and organization need out of this collaborative organization?

- What does your community and organization need to happen in the strategy developed to address the problem area?

- What do you need to be an effective member of this collaborative?

- Who is managing the resources? What kinds of accountability measures do you need?

- Is what you propose to do an effective use of your time?

- Will your stakeholders support you in this direction?

- And thousands more!

The community representation function is often described as a stewardship role. A steward protects the resources entrusted to it on behalf of the community. In the case of a collaborative, the governing body—usually a steering committee—is entrusted with the resources of the member agencies (which at first might be just the staffing costs of participants), which as public bodies manage public or foundation funds. Part of your role as a member of the collaborative is to ensure the wisest and best use of any resources.

The Leadership Function
The leadership work in governance is decision-making. It includes the activity of participating in the decision-making processes and also includes the activities of urging others to make decisions or saying that a decision or policy is needed. The

leadership function involves decision-making around priorities and outlining the allocation of physical, human, and financial resources.

When a decision is being discussed repeatedly, good governance practice says it is time to develop a policy to streamline the decision. For instance, if you specify in your terms of reference that the collaborative will hold its monthly meetings the first Monday of every month, you will save time and reduce the frustration of trying to come with a new date after every meeting. You do not want or need to have all the organizational policies of an autonomous NPO. The art of governance comes from determining which policies are critical and at what point.

Monitoring and Evaluation Function

This third leg of the function stool is really very important but is often neglected because it requires a lot of thought, good intentions, and resources to make it happen. Monitoring is not difficult, but regular reports to the decision-making body are also required to fulfill the role. If there are limited staffing resources, then the leadership must rely on verbal reports. This can still be done, albeit less effectively, as there is no paper trail. Evaluating program effectiveness needs to be initiated at day one. The next chapter provides guidance on how to evaluate the effectiveness of the process and the programming intervention. Another aspect of this function is the monitoring and evaluation of the senior staff person's performance, who then evaluates any other staff. If your collaborative has a manager and staff, then the intervention gets implemented primarily through their performance objectives and work plans. Monitoring and evaluating their performance provides data to determine whether the plan is being implemented and how it is working.

One last tool for decision-makers in a governance role is to monitor and evaluate themselves and their outputs. As with well-developed boards of directors, it is wise to regularly review your policies. Board audits are process evaluations for governing boards. If you are a long-standing collaborative with a substantive policy framework, you can use a board audit tool to review your work. The tool outlined in the next chapter is a good start.

What is policy-making?

A policy is a guideline and statement of values and principles to guide an organization's decision-making. It can instruct those performing the governance role, the senior staff, or any staff or volunteer working in that organization. A policy is a general statement of a decision-making body's beliefs on a certain matter, and states what it believes, values, and desires in approaching that matter. In addition, a policy forms a clear basis for the development and implementation of regulations and procedures. It provides direction, but does not prescribe methods for arriving at the result. A policy permits board and staff to interpret it in such a way as to adjust for changing conditions without making basic changes in policy. Well-developed policy includes performance metrics and a monitoring framework.

To intervene on a policy level means you are attempting to influence the behaviour of a system to achieve certain objectives. Policies describe WHAT to do. Procedures (or protocols) describe HOW to do it. Some policies, especially those developed for front line staff, incorporate the procedures and protocols (the methods) after specifying the desired outcomes and actions. These types of policies and procedures are found in an operational policy manual. Generally the development of procedures is the responsibility of operational staff and supervisors. But if you have few or no staff, the steering committee may need to develop operational procedures for its work. Policies set the boundaries for the principal activities of the organization and guide decision-making.

Why do collaboratives need policy?
Policies are developed when an issue repeatedly occurs and members need to systemize or standardize how to address a problem. Policies can address anything from recruiting strategies to spending restrictions. Policies also provide a framework for governance. Decisions recorded in a policy format can be used in similar situations without having to make other policy decisions. Policies permit decision-making to be objective, consistent, and transparent. Policies are living documents that can be amended to meet new challenges or to incorporate improvements. Collaboratives must decide what kinds of policies are relevant for them and their work. A collaborative may not need a complete policy framework such as those found in a standard NPO, but it may need a few pertinent policies to guide its interventions or programs. Policies generally guide the day-to-day work for financial activities, HR systems, and program management activities, but also provide guidance for the governing work of organizational decision-making, strategic planning, and growth.

Who says that a policy is necessary?
A sub-committee of the primary decision-making body or the senior staff person can be given the task of drafting a policy that will be considered and approved by the decision-making body. Anyone at a decision-making meeting can raise the

issue that a policy is needed, but the entire decision-making body must ultimately rule on the need for and appropriateness of the proposed policy.

When do you make policy?
A policy should be developed when an issue arises again and either the staff or decision-makers need to systemize or standardize how to address a problem. To build the capacity to govern the activities for the collaborative, the steering committee needs to put governance related policies in place. Not all these governance-related policies may be necessary at first, but as the collaborative begins to mature, secures resources, and moves into implementation of what was agreed to, terms of reference need to be reviewed, updated, and modified into full-blown policies.

Examples of governance related policies include:

- mission statement and or constitution

- methods for planning and developing goals and objectives

- procedural processes including decision-making and policy change processes

- collaborative organizational structure

- roles, responsibilities, and functions of the decision-making body, committees, and senior staff

- annual budgeting processes

- conflict of interest guidelines

- risk management procedures

- the role and authority of the senior staff person

- recruitment and orientation processes for new collaborative members

- meeting management guidelines

- evaluation and performance monitoring and accountability processes through reports to key stakeholders

- provisions for leadership in transitional phases and critical events

Once programs are in development or running, any resources used in day-to-day activities need direction from those who make governance decisions. At this point, the collaborative needs to develop policies to guide staff's day-to-day work. Policies that focus on daily operations are called operational policies. Examples of strategy or operational related policies:

- financial stewardship

- human resources stewardship

- program management

- risk management through policy and budget

How do you make policy?
The work of policy-making happens in meetings where proposals are put before decision-makers, questions are asked, and then decisions are taken. Ideally, board policy-making and adoption involves a number of inter-related steps.

Steps in the Policy Development Process[15]

STEP 1: DEFINE THE ISSUE OR PROBLEM
The process of policy development begins with recognizing the need for written policy. Decision-making bodies or staff often face decisions that would be easier to make if a policy existed. Sometimes an accreditation body or a funder will require a policy.

STEP 2: GATHER NECESSARY INFORMATION ON THE ISSUE
This step involves obtaining information from a variety of sources, such as:

- sample policy language and analysis from other organizations or collaboratives

- provincial or federal laws and regulations

- experience from other areas

- research

- local input

- workshops or seminars

Once facts are available, the decision-making body listens to recommendations for handling the policy issue. The senior staff person is often charged with

---

[15] The steps in the policy development process were adapted from the policy development steps at http://www.nsba.org/sbot/toolkit/PolSteps.html.

recommending policy action, since he/she is the one responsible for carrying out the policy.

STEP 3: REACH AGREEMENT ON THE FACTS AND OBJECTIVES
If the decision-making body can reach agreement on its objectives, then the policy options will be limited to the agreed-upon objectives. This limits the extent of the research, consultation input, and discussion.

STEP 4: ANALYZE ALTERNATIVES AND DEVELOP RECOMMENDATIONS
This step involves analyzing the alternatives and developing recommendations, including:

- Identifying alternative solutions and what instruments and resources are available

- Undertaking a thorough and systematic analysis of those alternatives

- Considering whether stakeholder/public consultation is necessary

- Engaging in consensus/compromise building with stakeholders or communities

- Developing recommendations to the board

- Presenting a report from the senior staff person or from an ad hoc committee

STEP 5: DISCUSS AND DEBATE RECOMMENDATIONS AT THE DECISION-MAKING LEVEL
At this point, decision-makers discuss the information and debate the following questions:

- Is the content of the recommendations within the scope of the decision-making body's authority?

- Is it consistent with municipal, provincial/state, and federal law?

- Does it support the collaborative's goals or objectives?

- Is it good practice?

- Is it reasonable? (Are any requirements or prohibitions arbitrary or discriminatory?)

- Does it adequately cover the subject?

- Is it limited to one policy topic?

- Is it consistent with the board's existing policies?

- Can it be administered? Is it practical? How much will it cost?

STEP 6: DRAFT POLICY
After the board has reached consensus on policy content, a policy writer (senior staff member or collaborative member) goes to work. This person must be able to write clearly, directly, and succinctly. Pomposity, verbosity, educational jargon, and legalese should be avoided unless necessary to meet legal requirements. A policy should be drafted loosely enough to leave room for adjustment to fit special circumstances.

STEP 7: ADOPT POLICY
Once in writing, the policy draft is placed on the decision-making body's agenda for a first reading, giving notice that the committee has a specific policy under consideration. The decision-making body then has the opportunity to discuss the proposed policy and, if it chooses, it may hold a public hearing. This is a good step for important or controversial draft policies.

STEP 8: MONITOR COMPLIANCE WITH POLICY
Policy oversight is a dynamic process that includes an evaluative component. Oversight makes sure that the policy accomplishes its goal. Policy oversight can provide guidance on whether to continue or modify the policy and to determine future courses of action. Monitoring can include a request for periodic reports from the senior staff. Be sure to define the timeframe.

STEP 9: POLICY EVALUATION AND REVISION OR MODIFICATION
You should review policies on a regular basis as a part of the decision-making body's standard operating principles. They can become out-of-date, unclear, or even contrary to the way in which the collaborative is operating. When any of this occurs, the policy needs to be modified or eliminated. The policy amendment process is the same as the policy adoption process. The decision-making body sets policy and the staff implements the policy and manages the programs within the guidelines set forth in the collaborative's policy. In the absence of policy, the staff must use their judgment.

Components of a Policy
Policies have a number of components, as indicated below.

Purpose – Why do you need a policy?

Goals and Objectives – What do you want the policy to accomplish?

Principles and Values – What principles and values are guiding the design and application of the policy?

Define the Problem – Is there a specific problem that is happening or anticipated? If so, make it explicit (e.g., to have checks and balances over the spending of money in this organization, we will require two signatures on every cheque).

Definition – Define any technical terms.

Procedures – Provide detailed expectations and commitments for each objective.

Accountability – Spell out who has the role of enforcing the policy. What will be the consequences if the policy is not complied with? Identify an appeal mechanism if possible.

There are two kinds of policies. The first supports the work of governance by the collaborative, and the second supports the work of managing the work and resources of the collaboration. Good policy reflects the organization's values and beliefs and is a general statement of a decision-making body's beliefs on a certain matter. The policy wording tells what and why certain things are wanted and forms a clear basis for the development of and implementation of rules and procedures.

See Appendix C for a sample policy development format and Appendix D for a sample communications policy.

Trustee or Lead Agency Arrangements
It is almost impossible to apply and receive funding for programs as an unincorporated organization. As a result, collaboratives often turn to an incorporated body of some sort under which they can apply for funding. This incorporated agency can be a non-member or a member of the collaborative. I use the terms *trustee* and *lead agency* interchangeably to describe the role, which can be as broad as the party's negotiate. The most narrow function of a trustee is usually to apply for funding (by signing proposals) and act as the financial administrator of that funding. The role at its most broad can include acting as the leader of the collaborative by chairing the collaborative, acting as employer to any staff, and managing the day-to-day activities of the collaborative through its own organizational infrastructure.

The collaborative may not need its own autonomous policies if it engages in a lead agency/trustee or fiscal sponsorship arrangement. The collaborative may choose to operate more as a program advisor and adopt the existing governance structure of the agency under which to operate. Instead of developing its own policies, the collaborative can choose to adopt the policies of the trustee. Be sure to spell out which ones you are adopting.

However, a collaborative will often have unique needs to fulfill, and a traditional non-profit organizational policy may not fit the bill. For instance, in the situation of a health promotion collaborative that is undertaking a behaviour change campaign, there may be the need to have collaborative members approve the key messages of the campaign. A protocol for this approval is needed in the collaborative's communication policy, and such a process is unlikely to be found in a regular NPO communication policy. The collaborative must add to the existing policy structure or come up with an additional policy framework on top of its trustee's framework.

Difficulties with a Trustee Relationship
A trustee or lead agency may be highly conscious of the risk and legal responsibility involved, leading it to demand that the collaborative focus on oversight and bureaucracy (at what may feel like the expense of programming). In addition, if there is a fuzzy decision-making protocol, the lead agency may assume much of the decision-making power and leave little for the collaborative to resolve. An unclear role for the trustee can lead to distrust and passivity on the part of the other collaborative members.

If an unincorporated collaborative chooses to engage a trustee or fiscal sponsor, it should address a number of issues in a separate agreement between the collaborative and the trustee, including:

- Determine how the collaborative will meet the trustee's organizational standards for financial management record keeping and managing staff.

- Decide how to manage the risks of complying with funding requirements. Will the trustee be full member of the collaborative, or can the trustee meet with staff on a regular basis and just supervise the systems and management practices through reports from the senior staff?

- Determine how the trustee will be involved in the relationship with funders.

- Settle on a fair amount of compensation for the trustee/fical sponsor role.

- Identify the role of the trustee agency in policy development (roles and responsibilities vis-à-vis the steering committee).

- Describe the legal responsibility of the trustee's board of directors.

All of these issues should be negotiated and formalized in a written agreement between the trustee or fiscal sponsor and members of the collaborative. Try to project into the future and envision what kinds of issues might arise, and develop specific processes or remedies to deal with these potential conflicts. The best resource for exploring and developing the trustee/collaborative relationship is Partnership-Trustee Journey: *A Handbook for Community Agencies in Partnership* by Anne Gloger. [16]

Components of a Collaborative Agreement

A partnership agreement amongst the members of the collaborative can be used when a group has moved past Step 4 and has a vision and action plan. The action plan is sometimes also called a strategy, and will determine much of the form the organization needs to build. This principle is similar to the "form follows function" principle used in architecture. It is difficult to develop an organizational structure until the strategy has been agreed to. For instance, if the strategy requires an autonomous structure to manage a lot of staff, the organization will require human resource policies and procedures and a mechanism to manage accountability. If the strategy requires an investment of funds that will be managed by only one partner, then less structure may be needed. Similar to the case of designing a building, we cannot design the structure of a collaborative until we know what is going to be happening within it.

Possible topics to cover in a collaborative agreement include:

- principles, beliefs, and values

- objectives/expected outcomes

- roles

- responsibilities

- benefits and acknowledgments

- process objectives/values

- mechanisms for conflict resolution and evaluation

- resources

[16] To order free copies of *The Partnership-Trustee Journey*, contact Anne Gloger at the East Scarborough Storefront in Toronto: email agloger@thestorefront.org or telephone 416-208-7853.

If you need something with more legal weight, see a lawyer about drawing up a legal contract. A sample collaborative agreement is found in Appendix E.

Drafting a Policy to Clarify Roles and Responsibilities

You may not know what roles members will play until after the vision is developed, but you can make a start at the first meeting of potential members and record what is agreed upon in the terms of reference. Members must understand their roles, rights, and responsibilities, and how to carry out their responsibilities. It is very common for NPOs to send junior staff to collaborative meetings to monitor activities, but not necessarily to participate whole-heartedly until they feel it will be productive for them personally.

When drafting any policy, consider brainstorming questions about the topic. Then use the sample format to organize the questions into the categories. Some questions to consider when drafting a roles and responsibilities policy include:

- What are the rules that determine who can be members, what they have to do to qualify, and what they need to do to maintain membership?

- Decision-making ability should be assigned by home organizations. What roles (staff, management or board member) are held by participants?

- Is it acceptable that representatives send alternates? Do you need any requirements and restrictions on the participation of non-members at meetings or group activities?

- How will order be kept in meetings? Will there be chairperson? If so, what other rights or responsibilities will the chairperson hold? Will there be other formal officers? If so, what will be their titles and responsibilities?

- Are there committees? What do they do and who is on them?

- How and when are officers, coordinators, committee chairs, and/or committee members selected, and how and for what cause can they be removed from their position?

- How will vacant positions filled?

- Who will take the minutes and distribute them? Who needs to approve the minutes prior to distribution?

- Does each member representative have a vote? What if two people from one organization attend a meeting?

- What is the member role in the collaborative? Is it to represent their home organization, represent a particular constituency, and/or represent themselves and their knowledge of the problem domain? Do they need to read the agenda and the minutes and correspondence to make informed decisions?

- Can the member representative participate in vision and direction setting events or do they need someone more senior? Does the completed strategy need home organization approval maybe even board adoption?

- Are members responsible for clarifying their home organization's positions on contentious issues?

Keep in mind that the governance framework needs to be flexible to ensure participation, but clarifying roles and responsibilities in a written document will help all the member organizations and their representatives determine how they can support the work of the collaborative. Some of the issues addressed above could be first developed into a terms of reference, and later translated into policies or a roles and responsibilities section of organizational bylaws or a collaborative agreement. The most important thing is to put it in writing and communicate the decisions and expectations to your members, both individuals and organizations.

Choosing a Decision-Making Tool:
There are two basic approaches to making decisions: consensus or some form of majority rules. It is most important that the group adopts a decision-making process in the terms of reference or bylaws and then sticks to it. Figure 14 shows a continuum of decision-making approaches.

Figure 14: Types of Decision-Making Approaches

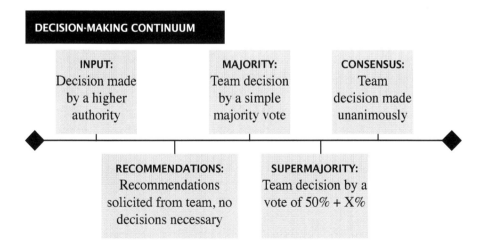

DECISION-MAKING CONTINUUM

INPUT:	MAJORITY:	CONSENSUS:
Decision made by a higher authority	Team decision by a simple majority vote	Team decision made unanimously

RECOMMENDATIONS:	SUPERMAJORITY:
Recommendations solicited from team, no decisions necessary	Team decision by a vote of 50% + X%

Recommendations:

The first step on the continuum does not involve the ability to make the decision, just to influence it. Situations that feel like collaborations because they involve many different stakeholders but do not hold the authority to make decisions are not really autonomous systems. Knowledge may be shared and transformed into a plan with recommendations, but the ultimate decision-making authority lies with another decision-making body. Ultimately, the recommendations may or may not get approved by the ultimate decision-making body. In saying this, I do not mean to denigrate this form of cooperation. In many cases the recommendations stand and are only modified by the higher authority.

Majority Rules:

This form of decision-making is the basis for voting procedures in parliamentary governments that have evolved out of the western democratic traditions. For a decision to be approved, the motion has to receive over 50% of the votes cast. Organizations and boards often use Robert's Rules of Order[17] to determine the proper procedures to manage meetings and casting votes.

Super Majority Rules:

This is a modification of the 50 plus one voting procedure. Many groups who want the benefits that come with higher numbers of support for a decision but resent spending the time to reach a consensus opt for a modified parliamentary procedure. Instead, they require 60% or 75% or more of the votes cast to support the subject motion.

Consensus Decision-Making:

Consensus decision-making does not mean unanimity where everyone has to wholeheartedly support the motion or course of action. It does mean that everyone has participated in the decision-making by putting their thoughts and concerns on the table, by exploring the various alternatives, and by collectively coming up with a course of action that everyone can live with and support. This form of decision-making expects differences of opinion and conflict is normalized. But it includes an element where one or more participants can block the process, thereby holding up the group indefinitely. Fear of this situation often motivates collaboratives to adopt a decision-making process that relies on consensus decision-making until a respectable time limit is met. Then the group falls back on modified majority rules for resolution.

Confidentiality: When is it an issue for collaborative decision-makers?

Confidentiality is often seen as dangerous territory in democratic decision-

---

[17] Some Canadian organizations are using Bourinot's Rules of Order (Fourth Revised Edition) based on the parliamentary rules used in the House of Commons in Ottawa.

making. Some advocate keeping discussions confidential and quiet to help create a positive group dynamic where members feel free to share their thoughts and feelings. However, there is established best practice and legislation in the case of government agencies, boards, and commissions when handling confidential issues. When confidentiality is clearly required, the decision-making body can elect to hold a closed confidential portion or part of a meeting. This part of a meeting is called in *camera*. Only those with the right to vote or participate in discussions are present. In camera discussions are supposed to be confidential and can be restricted ethically and legally.

In camera meetings generally deal with personnel issues, real estate negotiations, and any discussion of the collaborative's position in legal actions. For example, if a collaborative hires and manages staff, then the hiring and performance evaluation of senior staff are reasons to have an in camera meeting (assuming the senior staffer manages and hires junior staff). Purchasing or leasing space is another example. If a collaborative has resources to manage like property and staff, it is a good practice to develop a signed code of ethics specifying and prohibiting activities of decision-makers that breach confidentiality. These are all legitimate reasons for decision-makers to go in camera without the collaboration manager present.

Extroverted people in particular often think out loud and share opinions before they are fully formed. If members share points and positions during decision-making in the enthusiasm of a group discussion, it may not fair to represent the person who made a remark outside of the group. It is better for members of decision-making bodies to speak with one voice outside of the decision-making table and relate the decision to outsiders, not the discussion that occurred around decision-making. Given the above, it is important for organizational representatives to share any misgivings that may exist about a proposal under discussion. It is not fair to anyone to go along with the discussion and decision and then run back home and raise an alarm. This creates a high level of conflict that need never have happened and makes everyone look bad. However, unless the topics meet the criteria for in camera meetings, there is no need to restrict confidentiality.

Step 5 can be the most labour-intensive phase in developing a governance framework for a collaborative. This chapter explored the three functions of governance and the importance of developing policies to systemize decision-making and resolve recurring conflict. Governance arrangements can be streamlined by adopting a trustee to provide oversight and a governance framework to manage the collaborative's resources. This chapter also presented choices regarding decision-making tools and emphasized the importance of confidentiality in particular circumstances.

CHAPTER 10 STEP 6: EVALUATION—
Is the collaborative doing its work effectively?

If you have knowledge, let others light their candles in it—Margaret Fuller

Step 6, evaluation, is the final phase and can complete the entire process or begin it anew in whatever form the members decide. It can be a step to reflect on whether to continue the partnership, and can occur at the end of a project lifecycle but is not necessarily the end of the life of the collaborative. Collaboratives can evaluate at various points throughout their lifespan, including at the end of a project or a funding cycle or when external events spark a need to assess current programs.

This chapter explores what evaluation looks like, its value as a learning tool for the collaborative and others, and the difference between process and outcome evaluation. A tool for process evaluation is provided and the chapter presents the principal method for outcome measurement, a logic model. The chapter also provides some useful advice on using consultants and concludes with a discussion of evaluation as a governance function.

All groups ebb and flow, achieve goals, then define new directions. Some collaboratives dissolve and permit something new to arise out of the ashes. The capacity built with member organizations and individuals always makes it possible for organizations to transform into new processes and strategic plans.

Although evaluation is at the end of the step-by-step framework, an effective evaluation phase must include preconditions for success early on into the process. You need to develop measureable goals and objectives in Step 4 of the planning phase to evaluate the outcomes of the project, program, or strategy in Step 6.

Checking in on the group process is another form of evaluation and can take place at any point.

What is evaluation?
Evaluation is essentially a process to measure performance. In the NPO sector, most practitioners use the term evaluation to describe *program evaluation*, which focuses on discovering whether a program did what it set out to do in a proposal to its funder. A focus on the bottom line (profits and shareholder value) usually drives the private sector's evaluation efforts, although the movement toward corporate social responsibility aims to change that.

Key evaluation questions include:

• What is the purpose of the evaluation?

• How will the evaluation be used?

• What will you know after the evaluation that you don't know now?

• What actions will you be able to take based on evaluations findings?

What is the value of evaluation to collaboration projects?
Butterfoss and Francisco (2004) say that if a coalition is to succeed, evaluation must demonstrate a sustainable infrastructure and purpose, programs that accomplish their goals, and measurable community impacts. They propose a three-level evaluation model:

Level 1: Coalition infrastructure, function, and processes

Level 2: Coalition programs and interventions

Level 3: Health and community change outcomes

This is a great model for evaluation; it includes a process evaluation, a program evaluation, and an assessment of the collaborative's impact on the broader environment and stakeholders.

Collaboration practitioners conduct program evaluation in the same way that an agency delivers a program. A properly designed program has identified goals, objectives, and outcomes, and is organized into a logic model format or something similar. It makes no difference whether a sole service provider or a collaborative delivers the program when measuring progress to goals. As with any evaluation in human services, it can be very difficult to make clear causal links between one program's services and the ultimate successful outcome of individual, organizational, or social change. The difficulty is to draw the clear connection between your agency's services and the change experienced by the individual. Does someone have a job because of the employment agency's provision of job coaching and resumé services, or is it because of the childcare services provided down the street?

Program evaluations are rare and outcome evaluations of programs undertaken by collaboratives are almost non-existent in the NPO sector (Boutillier et al, 2007; Zizys, 2007). Collaboratives need to be more diligent in obtaining program evaluations so that the case can be made for the work of their service delivery. After all, the evaluation of projects adds to the credibility and reputation of an organization. Proper evaluation takes time and resources and is best planned at the beginning of a project. As well, because of their wide-raging nature, collaboratives cut across a broader range of issues and domains than just program delivery. Level 3 evaluations seek to identify the broader impacts on public health and safety, changes to delivery systems, community awareness, behaviour, and policy change. These changes may not have been overt goals for the collaborative, but are the result of the networked knowledge and coordinated behaviour of many players in a system.

Due to the length of time and investment of financial resources required for Level 2 and 3 evaluation, measuring intervention outcomes and community change (Level 1 evaluations) to assess the coalition functioning tend to dominate the academic literature. Program targets and system changes may occur, but it is difficult to demonstrate a clear cause and effect relationship.

Some authors argue that we also may not be asking the right questions when evaluating collaborative activity. Margo Hittleman, author of *Discussion Guide For Community Practitioners: Community Work Today: How Do We Count Caring?*, found practitioners frustrated with the emphasis on measuring hard outcomes.

When I talk with people working in many different community-based organizations, they often say something like the following: "So much of our work is about caring for people and communities. It is long-term and relational. At the same time, we do want to demonstrate responsible stewardship of public funds and public trust. We want to show that our work is "efficient" and "cost-effective." And we want to be able to improve the work we do. But how do we measure impact so that both our funders and we can assess our work? How can we help our funders (and the public) understand the nature of the work we do? In short, how do we count caring?" (Hittleman, 2008) "

Evaluation Needs to be About Learning

If the work of social change is about caring, the work of evaluation needs to be about learning. All the system players tout this objective of learning for evaluation purposes. However, many practitioners resist formal evaluations because of the risk. Innovation requires failure, and in the private sector new product failures are expected as part of the product development cycle. However, in the NPO sector evaluations of new or established programs may be unable to establish a clear causal link with the program because of the complexity previously mentioned. Yet this lack of clarity is easily associated with failure in the funders' minds. If an organization's funding is at risk due to an evaluation, then the organization should do everything it can to make the outcomes of the evaluation as favourable as possible.

Mistakes and learning are not easily accepted in the government worldview that Jane Jacobs called the Guardian Mentality in *Systems of Survival*. In this culture, protecting the taxpayer's dollar is always the priority, hence the guardian-like behaviour in civil servants. In government culture, where politicians are held accountable for every dollar spent, mistakes can be costly in terms of political scandal, and put careers at risk. NPO funding by governments are one level removed from this culture, but the more government funding they receive, the more they are assimilated into the cultural norms of government. Saying all that, non-profit organizations and collaborations need to learn from their work. In an ideal world, evaluation would be a learning process where mistakes can be made and learned from, as shown in Figure 15.

Figure 15: The Evaluation Process

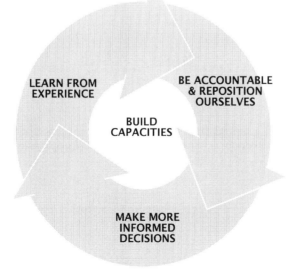

LEARN FROM
EXPERIENCE

BE ACCOUNTABLE
& REPOSITION
OURSELVES

BUILD
CAPACITIES

MAKE MORE
INFORMED
DECISIONS

There are a number of challenges associated with collaboration evaluation:

- It is hard to keep track of all the activities, especially when spread out across many partners.

- Partners have different capacities to gather data.

- Evaluation results can be highly political—failure or limited success can damage reputations with board members, volunteers, funders, and other key stakeholders.

- Evaluation can emphasize one type of evaluation over another (e.g., outcome over process/relational or vice versa).

- In the culture of urgency that exists in the NPO sector, it is difficult to make the room for program planning.

- Collaborative members may not have the skills or inclination to plan an evaluation in the start up phase of a collaborative.

- Evaluation findings can damage relationships by being used for outside or inside political purposes to assign blame or settle scores.

- A lack of accurate baseline measures and multiple influences may distort outcomes.

Difference between Process and Outcome Evaluation

Process evaluation focuses on group processes and the functioning of the organization. Since collaboratives are trans-organizational systems, you can assess their process as a quasi-organization. The evaluation of the process addresses the quality of member interaction and member satisfaction, how conflict is resolved and the sharing of power, and how organizational systems are functioning. In contrast, outcome evaluation looks at the impacts on, benefits to, and/or changes to your clients/target group as a result of your programming, projects, or behaviour change campaigns. Outcome evaluation can examine these changes in the short-term, intermediate-term, and long-term.

Process evaluation can include developing a process work plan for the group, whereas a process intervention might involve holding a skill building workshop in lateral leadership skills. A process evaluation can happen regularly; for instance, at the end of every meeting, the chair can ask for feedback about how the meeting went. A process evaluation can simply include three questions:

1. How is everything going?

2. What should we stop doing?

3. What should we start doing?

Process evaluation can also take place at regularly selected intervals and be more thorough. Assessing progress throughout a project allows you to take corrective action when and where it might be necessary. You can use the following tool to assess your current processes.

A Collaborative Process Assessment Tool
This tool is based on the six-step model for collaborative development first presented in *Alliances, Coalitions and Partnerships: Building Collaborative Organizations* and also used in this book. The model and this tool are adapted from the pioneering work of Thomas Cummings.

Choose a number from 1 to 5, with 5 representing the best performance of your collaboration in this area and 1 the worst. Place a checkmark in the box and then the corresponding number in the score box on that line. Once all topic areas are completed, tabulate your scores in the score box at the bottom of the assessment.

LEARN FROM EXPERIENCE	Did This Very Well	Doing/ Did This Well	Doing/ Did This O.K.	Doing/ Did This Poorly	(Did) Not Doing This	SCORE
STEP 1 DETERMINING THE NEED	5	4	3	2	1	
Catalysts – the collaboration was started because of existing problem(s) or the reason(s) for collaboration to exist required a comprehensive approach.						
Do our members, clients, and community people need us to address the issue?						
Are we gathering information from members, clients, and the community about their needs, wants, and preferences with respect to the organizing issue?						

LEARN FROM EXPERIENCE	Did This Very Well	Doing/ Did This Well	Doing/ Did This O.K.	Doing/ Did This Poorly	(Did) Not Doing This	SCORE
Are we constantly scanning the horizon for new information and developments with respect to the organizing issue?						
Do we have the expertise to deal with all aspects of the issue's complexity?						
SUBTOTAL						/25
STEP 2 MOTIVATION TO COLLABORATE						
There is a perceived need for the partnership in terms of areas of common interest and complementary capacity.						
Resources – the collaboration has access to needed resources (four types of capital: environmental, in-kind, financial, and human).						
There is a shared understanding of, and commitment to, the issue among all potential partners. The collaborative has developed to respond to the complex problem.						
The partners are willing to share some of their ideas, resources, influence, and power to address the issue.						
The perceived benefits of the partnership outweigh the perceived costs.						
SUBTOTAL						/25

LEARN FROM EXPERIENCE	Did This Very Well	Doing/ Did This Well	Doing/ Did This O.K.	Doing/ Did This Poorly	(Did) Not Doing This	SCORE
STEP 3 IDENTIFYING THE MEMBERS—WHO SHOULD BELONG?						
The partners share a common interest in the issue to commit to working though it.						
There is enough variety among members to have a comprehensive understanding of the issues being addressed and facilitate a shared learning approach.						
Partners have the necessary skills for collaborative action.						
There is a history of good relations between the partners.						
There is an investment in the partnership of time, personnel, materials, or facilities by all the members.						
SUBTOTAL						/25
STEP 4 COLLABORATIVE PLANNING						
There is a collective vision with clear goals a realistic action plan for the partnership. It is committed to by all partners.						
A neutral facilitator has led the group through this phase to ensure all partners are involved in planning and setting priorities for collaborative action.						

LEARN FROM EXPERIENCE	Did This Very Well	Doing/ Did This Well	Doing/ Did This O.K.	Doing/ Did This Poorly	(Did) Not Doing This	SCORE
The process has worked through it's purpose or mission and it is clear to our members and external stakeholders.						
Differences in organizational priorities, goals, and tasks have been addressed in the vision process.						
The action plan clearly shows objectives, tasks, responsibilities, and target dates for review and completion.						
SUBTOTAL						/25
STEP 5 **BUILDING AN ORGANIZATION**						
Trust building processes – members take pride in the way their work contributes to achieving the overall vision of our organization.						
There are strategies to ensure alternative views are expressed within the partnership. When conflict arises, the situation is handled respectfully and effectively to everyone's satisfaction.						
We regularly ask for feedback from our members about how well the organization is doing.						
If a project fails, or things go less well than planned, people learn from it and their readiness to continue to try new things is not diminished.						

LEARN FROM EXPERIENCE	Did This Very Well	Doing/ Did This Well	Doing/ Did This O.K.	Doing/ Did This Poorly	(Did) Not Doing This	SCORE
People feel comfortable to say what they think and feel, in a way that promotes problem-solving.						
SUBTOTAL						/25
Work coordination processes – the lines of communication, roles, and expectations of partners are clear.						
Partners have the task of communicating and promoting the coalition in their own organizations.						
Processes that are common across agencies, such as referral protocols, service standards, data collection, and reporting mechanisms, have been standardized.						
The administrative, communication, and decision-making structure of the partnership is as simple as possible.						
Processes that are common across agencies, such as referral protocols, service standards, data collection, and reporting mechanisms, have been standardized.						
The administrative, communication, and decision-making structure of the partnership is as simple as possible.						

LEARN FROM EXPERIENCE	Did This Very Well	Doing/ Did This Well	Doing/ Did This O.K.	Doing/ Did This Poorly	(Did) Not Doing This	SCORE
We keep up-to-date records on the organization, programs, activities, community needs, contact people, and resources available to our organization.						
SUBTOTAL						/25
STEP 6 EVALUATING EFFECTIVENESS						
The partnership can demonstrate or document the outcomes of its collective work.						
There are resources available from either internal or external sources to continue the partnership.						
Do enough people regularly attend full partnership meetings? There is a way of reviewing the range of partners and bringing in new members or removing some.						
There are regular opportunities to reflect on how things are done and how they could be improved.						
SUBTOTAL						/25

Tabulating Your Scores

Transfer the total from each category to the appropriate spaces below. (The highest total score you could have in any one category is 25.)

CATEGORIES:	SCORE
STEP 1 DETERMINING THE NEED	
STEP 2 MOTIVATION TO COLLABORATE	
STEP 3 IDENTIFYING THE MEMBERS—WHO SHOULD BELONG?	
STEP 4 COLLABORATIVE PLANNING	
CATEGORIES:	**SCORE**
STEP 5 BUILDING AN ORGANIZATION:	
• GOVERNANCE PROCESSES	
• WORK COORDINATION PROCESSES	
• TRUST BUILDING PROCESSES	
STEP 6 EVALUATING EFFECTIVENESS	
TOTAL SCORE	**/225**

Total Score:

150–225: Your collaborative organization is doing well.

100–149: This mid-range score suggests room for improvement. The partnership is moving in the right direction, but it will need more attention if it is going to be really successful.

0–99: Strongly suggests the need for improvement within your collaborative and signals the need to review whether there is collective will to address the issue at the present time.

Category Scores:

18–25: Everything is all right.

12–17: Indicates room for improvement.

0–11: Your collaborative definitely has work to do in this area!

Outcome Evaluation

Outcome evaluation is closely tied to the needs assessment and objective setting stages of your strategy or intervention developed in Step 4. An outcome evaluation simply measures how successful you were in meeting your objectives and assesses what has happened as a result of your work.

Principal Method for Outcome Measurement

The program logic model is a diagram in which stakeholders decide not only the program objectives, but also appropriate implementation steps. A logic model is good second step after developing a strategic plan. Groups take the strategic directions and goals and transform them into programs and projects with accountabilities, indicators, and milestones. Figure 16 shows the process involved in developing a logic model.

Figure 16: Logic Model Process

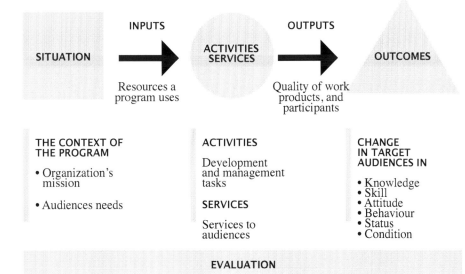

Using External Consultants

Program evaluation consultants are an excellent resource for outcome evaluations. As a neutral facilitator, they can gather feedback from members, member organizations, and community stakeholders. They often bring best practices to the table and their recommendations can improve your work while bringing objectivity to the outcome evaluation. A consultant is especially useful if you did not spend the time developing a program framework with program objectives and identifying anticipated outcomes. A program evaluator will work backwards to develop the program framework with accountability measures. It is more costly this way, but it is often the case as NPO programs get funding for evaluation after the fact.

Some evaluators try to bridge the gap between the paradigms that underpin the different forms of evaluation by avoiding applying goals to the process after the fact or in emerging situations, or emphasizing the perspectives of outsiders in designing evaluation strategies. One evaluator's attempt at meaning making in situations with fuzzy emerging processes, while at the same time decreasing the political pressure of evaluation, is Michael Quinn Patton's model called Developmental Evaluation.

As Table 6 demonstrates, there are important differences between traditional and developmental evaluation that make the latter particularly suited to emerging initiatives.

Table 6: Differences between Traditional and Developmental Evaluation

TRADITIONAL EVALUATIONS…	COMPLEXITY-BASED, DEVELOPMENTAL EVALUATIONS…
Render definitive judgments of success or failure	Provide feedback, generate learnings, support direction, or affirm changes in direction
Measure success against predetermined goals	Develop new measures and monitoring mechanisms as goals emerge and evolve
Position the evaluator outside to assure independence and objectivity	Position evaluation as an internal, team function integrated into action and ongoing interpretive processes
Design the evaluation based on linear cause–effect logic models	Design the evaluation to capture system dynamics, interdependencies, and emergent interconnections
Aim to produce generalizable findings across time and space	Aim to produce context-specific understandings that inform ongoing innovation
Focus accountability on and directed to external authorities and funders	Centre accountability on the innovators' deep sense of fundamental values and commitments
Uses accountability to control and locate blame for failures	Uses learning to respond to lack of control and stay in touch with what's unfolding and thereby respond strategically
Ensures the evaluator controls the evaluation and determines the design based on the evaluator's perspective about what is important	Ensures the evaluator collaborates in the change effort to design a process that matches philosophically and organizationally
Engenders fear of failure	Supports hunger for learning

Source: Patton, Michael Q. "Evaluation for the Way We Work." *The Nonprofit Quarterly*, Spring 2006, pp. 28-33.
Downloaded Feb 2, 2009 http://www.mcconnellfoundation.ca/default.aspx?page=139

Evaluation as a Governance Function

The work of evaluation as a governance function includes ongoing monitoring. Effective governance requires the form of evaluation discussed above. Yet a program evaluation takes place at one point in time, while monitoring and providing oversight of day-to-day activities happen on a continuous basis. Like evaluation, the focus of monitoring is to enhance the effectiveness of your efforts by establishing a clear link between past, present, and future decisions and results. The information from monitoring can be used to:

- ensure compliance with the funder's and the originating organization's expectations;

- fine tune decisions;

- shift course if the present course is not generating results; and

- help plan for the future.

A commitment to monitoring the activities of the collaborative reflects a commitment to continuous improvement. Without monitoring the progress of the work and the implementation of the plan or strategy, you cannot judge if you are getting where you want to go, determine whether you can credibly claim progress and success, or determine how to improve on your efforts.

How do you monitor?

Monitoring is the information gathering process by which decision-makers know what is happening with a policy or program. In other words, if policy designers (board members and executive director) are distant from the implementers (executive director and staff), they are constrained in their control of policy implementation. Ongoing monitoring of how the collaborative's plans and initiatives are developing is critical to the governance function. Monitoring is a way to provide feedback to collaborative members and staff on program delivery and resource allocation.

Monitoring tools include:

- performance reports from the executive director/collaborative manager

- regular financial reports

- annual reports

- program evaluation

- performance evaluation of the executive director/collaborative manager

- policy development and review community and stakeholder consultation

- benchmarking reports

- development of business plans

- self-audits by the collaborative decision-makers

- sharing and reviewing best practices

- attending sector conferences and events

- comparisons of statistics

Evaluation is the last step in the linear process of collaborative development, but it may not signal the end of the process. Instead, it might become a time for reflection and realignment with a continuation of the work. There are many benefits to using evaluation as a mechanism to learn about whether the processes, initiatives, and strategies did what they were intended to do or had some other impact. Evaluation of collaboratives is a complex task that can require process, outcome, and community impact forms of evaluation. Further to evaluation is the ongoing governance function of monitoring the processes and activities of the collaborative to ensure compliance with organizational policies and procedures and any other legal requirements that apply.

CHAPTER 11:
Rapid Development of Crisis-Driven Collaboratives

The Tao begot one, one begot two, two begot three.
The three begot the ten thousand things.
The ten thousand things embrace Yin and express Yang.
Harmony is achieved by combining these forces.—Lao Tzu 14

Communities around the world are facing unexpected calamities on a large scale. The developing world is often located in more weather-prone zones, have never stopped facing large-scale catastrophe, and have few resources to manage a crisis. Their large institutions are fewer and often managed by armed forces and international NGOs[18] rather than governments and local authorities. In contrast, the more developed world may start off with more emergency response and resources, but the more infrastructure a community has prior to a catastrophic event, the more damage it incurs and the higher the expectations of community members for a rapid coordinated response. The impact of the Katrina hurricane, which broke the levies around New Orleans, showed how we in the developed world are not as invincible as we want to believe.

We tend to expect governments to solve complex problems that they have little or no control over. Just recently the global economy imploded and the masses demanded that governments respond. No-one questioned how a single government could solve the problems of the global financial system when it had no legal jurisdiction or source of power to do so. Alas, voters do not care about this complexity—they just want a quick solution. As problematic as this is for

---

[18] NGO stands for non-governmental organization. The term is favoured is by international aid organizations instead of non-profit organization.

leaders, the moral imperative to act can become a source of amazing power and can justify overcoming stalemated systems. When the need to act is overwhelming and people are looking for leadership, organizing a collaborative can be an effective strategy. Collaboratives provide a way to deal with the complexity and aggregate the power of disparate and autonomous governments or organizations to achieve a coordinated response to an emergency situation. In this chapter we will explore a process framework to build trust quickly amongst organizational players coming together for an emergency response.

What do we know about rapid group development?
Groups move through stages of group development before they reach a place where they can work effectively and easily. You cannot get around it, so you need to expect it and plan for it. The answer is to move slower to move quicker. Chapter 7 introduced Will Schutz, a major organization theoretician, who proposed a three stage model of group development: inclusion, control, and affection. There are other theories of group development with similar stages, but this is the simplest. Groups always begin with an inclusion period where the need to belong to the group has to be satisfied. There is always a period of conflict where those with higher control needs jockey for leadership. Once the group has moved through these two stages, the members are rewarded with productive relationships that foster high performance. So, in a crisis, any new team—inter-organizational or not—has to move through these stages. The desired stage to be working in during crisis mode is the affection stage. If you have a crisis response team in place that has worked together, knows each other, and has experience resolving conflicts together, then they are primed and ready for action. If the group has not journeyed through the first two stages, then your task is to take them through these steps as quickly as possible.

The first meeting of a crisis-driven collaborative at the inclusion stage has several objectives:

• To provide safe ways to release the negative emotions and reduce adrenalin surges generated by a crisis

• To create a safe environment for multiple perspectives to be voiced and conflict to be normalized, and to work through the stages of group development as quickly as possible

• To create enough of a governance structure for transparent decision-making

• To scope out the complex problem by facilitating a puzzle learning process

• To determine enough key pieces of a strategy to get to the next stage of decision-making

The following chart shows a sample agenda for first meeting.

TIME	ACTIVITY
0–20 MINUTES	Introductions and icebreaker
20–30 MINUTES	Ground rules
30–45 MINUTES	Needs sharing: Laying the foundation for negotiation
45–60 MINUTES	Decision regarding decision-making process
60–110 MINUTES (50 MIN)	The Collective Brain Dump • Scoping the problem or assembling the group's intelligence • Reaching agreement on the problem • Deciding what decisions are needed • Deciding and action planning
110–120 MINUTES	Closing

This is a lot of work to do, but since it is a crisis, expect people to be willing to spend the time and energy to move forward. First, help the group along the inclusion stage by making group members feel welcome and included. This usually involves using some form of introduction and warm-up exercises called icebreakers. In a crisis situation the anxiety is even higher than normal amongst group members, so the activity really needs to help lessen this anxiety. However, ensure the sense of urgency does not overwhelm the process and prevent clear thinking. This sense of urgency is voiced by people saying things like, "We do not have time for process right now," "Don't waste time, we must act," or "Every minute is precious."

Despite the high anxiety, your leadership is needed to offset this stream of fear to create an environment for the group's emotions to be expressed and honoured. It is important to pay attention to process on the assumption that the group members have not worked together before. If people have worked together before and know and trust each other, you can spend less time on the inclusion stage, but you should still have some form of check-in to transition from the outside into the present moment with the group. Crisis breeds fear and anxiety, and decision-makers need to reduce these emotions. Structuring ways to do this in the meeting helps prevent the blowups that can come later on in the control phase of group development.

Icebreaker
One of my favourite icebreakers that allows negative feelings to be expressed is the *Hopes and Fears Icebreaker.* If you are leading the meeting, ask the participants to express either a hope or a fear about the process or the content of the meeting. Although the expression of hope might be seen as positive emotion, it also recognizes a situation that needs change. Record the hopes and fears on a flip chart and refer to them as you go along. This exercise establishes the habit of speaking the truth instead of sugar-coating the issues, and allows the process to move along with more alignment between what people are thinking and saying. Depending on the numbers around the table, this activity might take 30 minutes.

Ground Rules
The most important process task is to keep the group real, respectful, and engaged. With the prevalence of email and text messaging on cell phones, meeting participants often become totally disengaged from the work of the meeting. Crisis situations naturally provoke increased communication, and anxiety only heightens the need to control. Having the group agree to a rule about the use of cell phones may be prudent to maintain participant focus and concentration. Other ground rules could include group rules like one person speaks at a time, build on others' ideas, and there are no wrong answers/ideas or silly questions.

Laying the Foundation for Negotiation
The truth-telling modelled in the icebreaker leads nicely into the control phase of group development. Instead of avoiding it and pretending the divvying up of resources, credit, and prestige are not important, confront the control issue head-on. Ask participants to speak on behalf of their organization and inform the group what they need out of the process. For example:

• Do they need their reputation protected?

• Do they need help meeting their mission or role?

• Do they need part of the funding or resources that may come to the collaborative?

• Do they need to take credit for their involvement?

These issues will be very important to government representatives or politicians and will be on their minds throughout the meetings. Record the group's responses if they are not too politically sensitive. This activity may take up to 30 minutes, but probably a lot less. Do not let participants critique each other or assess the value of their needs. If participants say they need it, they do. Leave it at that.

By the time you are through this activity, the collaborative will have built enough trust so that people know they can be real and not have to posture. This should take less than one hour. You spent that hour building relationship capital because you need a certain amount of trust and honesty to move the group through the control stage as fast as possible. In Bruce Tuckman's group development model[19], this control stage is called storming (a more descriptive term to describe the debate that occurs). There is now enough investment in the group that people feel comfortable putting out their strong opinions and needs. Inevitably, these opinions and needs will conflict with others. Conflict is a normal part of group life. People and organizations hold different values and beliefs and serve different clientele and markets. Instead of going right into analyzing the problem, try to channel some of the turbulence into developing the least amount of governance structure you need at this point—primarily a decision-making process.

A Decision-Making Process
Everyone must agree whether decisions are going to be made by consensus or majority rules. The problem with consensus decision-making is that the process can be blocked by individual members and resolution can sometimes take a lot of time. Since time is of the essence in a crisis situation, expect major opposition to a consensus decision-making process. However, there is nothing stopping you from combining the two methods. Feel free to agree to make as many decisions as possible through consensus until a decision-making impasse is reached. Then have the group fall back to majority rules decision-making. A 50 plus one vote is probably not good enough, so adopt the rule that 75% of votes are needed to pass a controversial decision. A discussion about decision-making processes should take 15 minutes.

Another approach to deal with a decision-making impasse is to empower the group leader to make the decision. A leader/facilitator can let the group know that if they fail to make the decision within time limits, the leader will. This creates a need to move through the issue instead of avoiding the conflict.

Your group now has a process to resolve conflict. This permits you to move into areas of high conflict and deal with the crisis. Up until now you have been building the mechanism to deal with the crisis. Now you can start defining the

[19] Tuckman, Bruce W. (1965) 'Developmental sequence in small groups', *Psychological Bulletin*, 63, 384-399.

problem set. Instead of going around the table and letting everyone put in their two cents, create a structure to scope out the problem.

The Collective Brain Dump

In meeting conversations where people share their concerns and their experiences, usually all the contributed information is left to hang in the air. Some people will speak to what is happening, others to why, and others to how. When the data is unorganized, you create a competitive condition where everyone has to become an advocate for their particular piece of data to be included in the problem analysis or solution. There is usually no reason to set up competitive conditions because everyone has a piece of the puzzle you are trying to build, and their contributions (data) need to be thought of as pieces of that puzzle. A meeting leader's or facilitator's task is to decide where to put the pieces of the puzzle or the data contributions of the meeting participants.

One of the simplest structures for organizing the participants' contributions when scoping a problem is to use the five Ws and one H process as described by the six honest serving-men:

> I keep six honest serving-men
> (They taught me all I knew);
> Their names are What and Why and When
> And How and Where and Who.
> Rudyard Kipling, *Just So Stories* (1902)

Record all the data that people share under the five W and one H titles. The facilitator/recorder must know enough to make informed judgments about under which title the shared information should be placed. If the group thinks the recorder has made a misjudgment, they should call the recorder on it and discuss where it should be placed. One of the most important ways to express leadership as a meeting facilitator is to organize the data as the participants contribute it. This is seen as highly controlling by some facilitators, as organizing and categorizing the data is the facilitation tool to help the group reach consensus in their processes. Other approaches, such as Dynamic Facilitation, include the following categories: solutions, data, concerns, and problem statements. At the beginning of the meeting and as participants provide answers to the questions, the facilitator places the remarks with their agreement on the appropriate chart. If there is disagreement with one of the remarks, the disagreement is noted under the category of concerns.

In the same way, you can also use the steps in a simple problem-solving process as category titles to organize participant data. For example:

- understanding the problem or issue

- definitions and terms

- possible causes

- possible solutions

- criteria for decision-making

- action planning—the how

Whatever structure you choose, when all the pages are filled with ideas and pieces of information, you have data around which to build consensus and to discern where there are disagreements. Display these sheets on the wall or on large whiteboards in front of everyone.

A word about defining the problem/problem set: the boundaries of the problem set are determined by who is in the room. Marginalized people frequently see their problems defined as something that does not matter to them because well-meaning researchers come in, define their problems, and present solutions without ever consulting or involving them. Usually the proposed solutions are not related to what people think are their problems, so there is no commitment to implementing them. These well-researched reports then remain on the shelf; engineers use the term *garbage in, garbage out* (GIGO).

The same holds true in a group where the knowledge inputs are determined by who sits at the table and contributes. If a critical knowledge piece is missing, the problem and ensuing analysis will be flawed. Conversely, if you have the right knowledge pieces but the group does not encourage equal participation and contribution, the knowledge puzzle will again be flawed. This is why group dynamics are important. Process folks saw this borne out by the post-mortem analysis of the Challenger disaster undertaken by NASA. The Rogers Commission found that *NASA's organizational culture* and decision-making processes were key contributing factors to the accident.[20]

Convergence: Finding Common Ground
Decision-making might be obviously easy once you have organized participant contributions into a clear problem statement and possible solutions. Ideally, the group chooses the most promising solution or course of action and moves into the how. More than likely you will need to focus further discussion with each W or step until agreement is reached. Moving step-by-step, the facilitator/leader

[20] Rogers Commission was a special commission appointed by United States President Ronald Reagan to investigate the Challenger accident. The Rogers Commission Report (1987) can be found at http://history.nasa.gov/rogersrep/51lcover.htm

focuses the decision-making, then closes off discussion and moves on to the next W or step until an action plan is developed. This is highly-skilled facilitation work and my instructions are simply an introduction. These skills include the ability to keep calm under pressure, to keep the group focused and on track, to ensure the inclusion of those less inclined to barge into discussion, and to build agreement.

Building Agreement Techniques:
Have you noticed someone in your group who can nicely sum up an issue? Ask that person to sum up the data on the chart. Let the summary hang in the air for a minute or two as group members digest it. Ask group members whether they can live with that interpretation of the issue. If so, record it on a separate sheet of flip chart paper and post it for everyone to see. Continue in this manner until disagreements are raised. When there is a clear disagreement, ask for suggestions on how to resolve it. Allot a limited time for discussion and then present the options clearly to the group. If necessary, fall back on the decision-making process agreed to at the beginning of the meeting. Remember that conflict is normal— even desirable—and to get the group to work at its peak capacity you need to move to and through the control phase.

Decision Trees:
A *decision tree* is another method you can use for group decision-making. By organizing your information graphically, the group can make good choices, especially decisions that involve high costs and risks. Decision trees use a graphic approach to compare competing alternatives and identify best solutions for the information available. Figure 17 shows a sample decision tree.

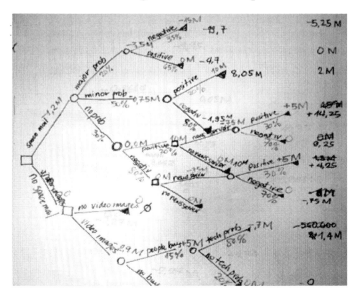

A decision tree consists of three types of nodes:

1. Decision nodes – commonly represented by squares

2. Chance nodes – represented by circles

3. End nodes – represented by triangles

A good primer on decision trees can be found at http://www.stylusandslate.com/decision_trees/

Since it is a crisis, action planning must occur. Maybe the time does not need to be spent on problem definition and problem solving. Often there are plans in place that need to be implemented in emergency situations. In that case, start by reviewing the plan. Ensure that each step is still feasible and that someone is responsible for that step. If decisions need to be made, record them on a flip chart. Once you have reviewed the plan, take the group's attention back to the decision list. If time is running out, prioritize the decisions that need to be made and ensure the group makes them before leaving. Is additional information needed to support the group's decision-making? If so, make sure the group decides who will get it.

Another process issue around decision-making is to ask whether there are others waiting on decisions by this committee. If so, what are they and what does the group need to make them? Use a chart to record the decisions and who is responsible for them. This chart will then form the structure for the next meeting.

Minutes/Worksheet

MEETING DATE AND TIME:			
PERSONS ATTENDING:			
DECISION TAKEN/ ACTIVITY	TIMEFRAME	PERSON RESPONSIBLE	COST/INPUTS

How to close the first meeting:

Regular meeting process requires asking the group if anyone has any other business or issues that need airing. Hopefully in an emergency situation no one has held anything back, but it is better to ask before closing the meeting down. Therapists have identified a phenomenon where clients spill their real concerns when they have their hands on the doorknob and are about to leave the room at the end of the session. Unconsciously, the client is fearful of bringing up the material and leaves it until the last minute. This phenomena happens in meetings too.

Be sure to ask if everyone understands their action items. An emergency situation is not the time for people to leave and come to the next one pleading ignorance. Ask people to stay behind if they need additional clarification. Finally, ask people how they are feeling. They should be feeling better than when they came into the meeting. Ask if everyone got what they needed. If you can hold them for a moment, ask them whether the meeting worked. Do they need items for the next meeting's agenda? Schedule the next meeting before people leave, or preferably use a fixed schedule for meetings.

Second and Subsequent Meetings

Subsequent meetings should carry on with the planning and decision-making started at the first meeting. If the plans are underway, focus on accountability and ensuring the work gets done, as well as removing roadblocks. It is always wise to begin meetings with a warm-up phase to help people transition into the group. It does not have to be a formal icebreaker, but you may wish to give everyone an opportunity to tell what is new and if there are any interesting tidbits of intelligence or urgent matters to discuss. As with the first meeting, you want people to feel safe and willing to freely share their thoughts and perspectives. Asking for agenda items at the beginning of the meeting loosens up the power from the chairperson, although if you were able to develop an action strategy in the first meeting, use that document to move through the agenda.

Crises are usually time limited. When the crisis is short-term, you may not need much more than a decision-making process for a governance structure. However, if decisions become repetitive, you may need to start developing policy. As well, if the committee is going to meet on a regular basis or morph into a long-term initiative, you need to work through the six-step framework.

You may have noticed that this process will work for any regular meeting or process. It is a good place to start, but as you progress you need more structure. As you manage many different initiatives, you might not want to oversee all the details of each project plan, but instead want reports that can be referred to in meeting minutes. The important learning from this chapter is that the group process must be attended to, even in times of crisis.

CHAPTER 12:
MANAGING CONFLICT AND POLITICAL DYNAMICS IN COLLABORATIVES

In the beginning is the relationship.—Martin Buber, I and Thou

Power in Collaboratives

Power is the energy to access resources and influence or make decisions. It is sourced in various ways. Power is neutral in terms of its goodness and can foster both positive and negative outcomes. In Western culture, many people think of power as a dirty word.

This chapter tries to reframe the notion of power as a negative force and instead presents power as neutral energy that is necessary for the collaborative to achieve its goals. The chapter explores the sources of power needed to help move or disrupt collaborative organizational processes. You will begin to acquire the ability to identify and address power issues and political tactics, and become comfortable with facilitating a group discussion about power. Conflict is the word most associated with power. The chapter continues the discussion of power by focusing on conflict in collaboratives, its inevitability and relationship to group dynamics, and what tools are available to the practitioner to manage it productively.

When a collaborative is formed by joining together the power of its individual members, the power of the collaborative is enhanced and there is more energy to tackle complex problems and social messes. By joining together with other organizations, you aggregate the legitimate power source of each agency. In doing so, however, there are unstated or unknown power sources in play, agency turf issues, and the ability to control resources that have the potential to morph into issues through the day-to-day functioning of collaboratives. As soon as other organizations and participants join the process, power issues emerge. As you identify potential participants, consider the sources of power they can bring to the process and any political dynamics that might arise.

Sources of formal power include:

• Formal authority-vested in positions and titles

• Control of scarce resources

• Use of structure, rules, and regulations

• Control of decision-making processes

• Control of knowledge and information/expertise

• Control of boundaries

• Control of technology

• Structural factors that define the stage of action

Sources of informal power include:

• Systemic power associated with class, ethnicity, race, and age

• Symbolism and the management of meaning

• Gender and the management of gender relations

• Personal power and confidence

• Charisma and/or the capacity to create fear in others

• An ability to communicate

• Interpersonal alliances, networks, and control of informal organization

• Ability to cope with uncertainty
(Roberts, 2004, p. 60)

Power issues are best addressed as soon as possible in the development process to prevent future conflict. How do you do this? First, honour the self-interest of all parties from day one. All participants in a group process seek to promote or protect their organizational and often personal interests. Some people describe these interests as hidden agendas, making them sound quite negative. Altruism is a dominant value within the NPO sector. Because working from one's self-interest is the opposite of operating from the common good, there is often an unspoken norm in meetings that dampens honest discussion about what people and organizations want and need when working together. If nothing else, organizations work to preserve themselves and need to ensure collaborative activities do not damage them. When you can accept this, accepting that organizations want to enact their mission and even expand their service delivery is totally reasonable as well. By accepting self-interest as a principal motivator of the partnership members by openly discussing needs and wants, you can use honest discussion to negotiate a new organization into being. Not everyone will get what they want, but hopefully members will get what they need. Although self-interest is the place to begin, to continue you need to transcend differences and move toward finding common ground so you can collaborate and work together.

Interests are not the same as demands or positions. Demands and positions are what people say they must have, while interests are the underlying reasons, needs, or values that explain why they take the positions they do. For instance, if your organization has a grassroots constituency, it will be in your organizational self-interest to further their interest because your organization is aligned with that constituency. You will want to protect that constituency throughout the evolution of the collaborative. There is nothing dishonourable about that. Even if it is only you (whether you are the convenor or not) who summons the courage to say what you need and want to get out of this grand experiment of working with the others, you will be modelling honesty and openness and others will emulate it when they feel safe enough.

From day one, everyone needs to be clear about individual organizational needs. If the direction of the collaborative veers from what is best for a specific constituency, everyone will know the member will speak up or probably walk away if the direction is harmful for that constituency. Your agenda is not hidden; it is clear and simple and everyone understands your organizational boundaries. In addition, potential conflict is averted because everyone knows where you stand and will not make assumptions about what position you will take.

Once everyone knows where other organizational interests lie, negotiation can take place between the various positions members are likely to take on issues. In fact, even before active negotiations can take place, members will take action to accommodate differing organizational interests and positions to avert future conflict. However, if you have not had frank discussions about power and interests, assumptions will be made that will very likely lead to conflicts. As the old saying goes, prevention is worth a pound of cure.

A Common Scenario

Anytown Foodbank decided that to further their mission of serving the needy, they had to do more than just run a food bank. The organization decided to provide additional social services to their clients to complement the existing food service. However, they were wary of stepping on the toes of the other agencies in town. One of the biggest agencies was a Riverbank multi-service agency that provided social services to their clients. This agency thought they should be in charge of the food bank and had told this to the United Way. These two agencies were now invited to participate with other community agencies in a new funding partnership for homelessness prevention. The funding deadline was in two weeks. All the agencies around the table knew there was a storm brewing between the Anytown and Riverbank agencies, but everyone subconsciously agreed there was no time to openly discuss the conflict. The content of the conversation focused on platitudes like, "Just focus on the client," and "Let's just get the money and then we'll figure out who gets what."

What do you think will happen in this scenario? Is the groundwork laid for healthy and productive working relationships?

To facilitate a personal reflection or a group discussion about power, ask the following questions:

• What kinds of power does each organization/person source?

• What do you know that gives you power?

• What do you know that no-one else knows?

• What would make you eager to share your knowledge?

• What would you share and what wouldn't you share?

• Do you risk anything when you share knowledge?

• What level of involvement should each member have, especially about decision-making?

• What are the influences on the system? Who has the power to influence what you do?

• What supports/structure do you need to share knowledge, skills, processes, motivation/attitudes, environment, opportunity, culture, and power?

Keep this in mind: Power is not only what you have, but what others think you have!

Power and Political Tactics

There is no more engaging and volatile aspect of work life than organizational politics. In most places, people are not comfortable openly discussing politics. Politics in organizations is like sex was in the 1950s—people knew it was going on, but nobody talked about it. In fact, the first rule of politics is that nobody tells you the rules. That way, the lucky ones can play a game that others cannot figure out.

Power is the capacity and influence is the tactic that you use. When you are facing a unique situation on a matter that is quite important to you, you tend to use the tactic you are most comfortable with. Political tactics in organizations include:

• manipulating situations and at times people

• managing information and plans carefully to your own advantage

• invoking the names of high-level people when seeking support for your projects

• becoming calculating in the way you manage relationships

• paying great attention to what people above you want from you

• living with the belief that to get ahead, you must be cautious in telling the truth

The same behaviour can be seen in collaboratives. In this case, manipulation can include:

• being indirect, clever, closed

• saying what you do not mean

• name dropping

• expressing only one side of the story—understating the downside

• using persuasion techniques

• padding your demands

• using language that masks reality (e.g., the Fair Rent Act)

Manipulation is behaviour undertaken by those operating from a power-under position. Those in a power-with relationship search for win–win solutions, while those in a power-over situation bark orders at those unlucky enough to have to follow them. If a collaborative is operating in a democratic mode, the underlying power structure should be power-with. If it is hierarchical, it is operating using power-over and power-under structures.

Positive Political Skills

Power and politics can be really positive. Many people, especially women, assume that power and politics are dirty business and therefore tend to stay away from using their expert power or their authority. And yet, if you are in a power-over situation (e.g., you are the boss), sometimes people just want you to say, "I'm the boss and I think this is the best thing for us to do under these circumstances." In personal relationships, the essence is to exchange feelings. However, at work— and especially in collaboratives—the most productive meetings involve saying, "Here is what I want from you. What do you want from me?" This is the skill of negotiation, which is the most useful political skill in any group.

To get your own house in order in terms of power, do the following:

- be your own authority—state what you believe and why

- say no when you mean no

- share as much information as possible

- disclose your own vulnerability

- participate and encourage others to participate in decision-making

- use language that describes reality, name that reality, identify your part in it, and state what you want from others

You can help others express their power by:
- encouraging self–expression and accepting others' feelings, wants, desires, and enlightened self-interest

- making commitments instead of sacrifice

- staying focused on who you want around you

- acting in ways that give others around you ownership

- discouraging and confronting passive, non-assertive behaviour

Do power and conflict go together?

Power and conflict are very often correlated and interdependent, but they do not have to be. Peers with similar sources of power can be engaged in conflict over ideas, and sometimes egos carry a conflict further than it ever needed to go. Even when power is not at the root of the conflict, one or both of the parties wants the power to influence the course of events. One person or organization has to feel disempowered in some way to initiate a conflict.

If there is a power imbalance, perceived or real, and a collaborative member holds negative feelings about it, the possibility of conflict is high. I am not saying that all situations or organizations need to have power sharing or equity at all points in time. One person can have more power at any point in time, if everyone else is fine with that. When others seek to hold that power, dynamics need to be resolved or they will undermine the very survival of the collaborative.

There are lots of political dynamics outside the collaborative that you may need to engage in, but for this discussion I will focus on internal political dynamics. Some dynamics can be resolved with an effective governance structure. Widely-accepted policies reduce the potential for conflict. Organizational capacity is developed and people become more comfortable knowing there are ways to deal with conflict in a positive manner. For instance, if the collaborative is engaged in a conflict over who gets to speak on behalf of the collaborative, the solution lies in the collaborative developing a communications policy. To do that, you first have to honestly deal with the issue. Brainstorm a list of questions to answer, such as:

- What do members need to have confidence in a spokesperson?

- Does the spokesperson have to follow an approved message?

- Does the spokesperson need to be articulate and a good speaker to state the case succinctly for the media?

- Do the collaborative members need to refrain from sharing their own opinions or representing their own organization?

- Is there a lot of profile to be gained from being a collaborative's spokesperson?

- Who wants a chance at it?

- Can the position be shared, or is it better to invest in developing one person?

- Is it best for the spokesperson to hold the chair position so he/she appears to have authority?

Once you answer these questions, assemble the answers together into a communications policy that will guide the group into the future. A sample communication policy is provided in Appendix D.

Not all conflict can be easily dealt with. People are often very afraid to be honest. One of the most widely repeated truisms in our culture is that honesty does not pay. Whistleblowing legislation is needed to protect civil servants who expose corruption. Is it any wonder that witnesses to unethical and dishonest behaviour stay quiet when there may be many incentives to close ones eyes and say nothing? If you are trying to create a participative culture in your collaborative and need people to be honest, you have to ensure there are no disincentives that prevent honesty. You might even try to be proactive and reward people for it in some way. Certainly, modelling honesty is the best way to encourage it. Some things might be painful to hear, but what is hidden can undermine the whole process. Over time, with honest sharing, you can build trust and the barriers will come down.

Conflict and Group Dynamics

Schutz's theory, first introduced in Chapter 7, provides a model to use to predict group dysfunction. As stated earlier in the first stage of inclusion, if people do not feel welcomed at the beginning of the process, you can trigger negative attitudes and disengagement. At the control stage, conflict is predictable and even desirable. You do not get to the productivity stage (affection) unless you move through the conflict stage. The key learning for collaboratives is not to avoid the inevitable, but to manage it well. A governance structure that includes a decision-making process goes a long way to legitimizing the different perspectives of collaborative members, and provides one mechanism to work through conflict. A policy-making focus helps to organize and channel the conflict. In the last stage of group development, where most of the work gets done, Schutz emphasizes that inter-personal relationships are the glue that holds the collaborative together. By fostering relationships and accepting conflict as normal, you will be rewarded with high productivity.

Keep in mind that with every new group member, the group reverts back to the inclusion stage. If the membership is ever-changing, the group dynamics may never move past the inclusion phase. This happens very frequently in collaboratives, and the group never moves through to the conflict stage. The group's work becomes including newcomers and little knowledge transformation takes place.

Firo B: A Measure of Needs

Shutz also developed a tool to determine these needs on a personal basis. The Fundamental Interpersonal Relations Orientation-Behavior (FIRO-B) questionnaire measures an individual's orientation toward six interpersonal needs. Table 7 describes this model.

Table 7: The Firo-B Six-Cell Model and Behaviours

INCLUSION	CONTROL	AFFECTION
EXPRESSED INCLUSION: • Talking and joking with others • Involving others in projects and meetings • Recognizing others' accomplishment • Incorporating everyone's ideas and suggestions	**EXPRESSED CONTROL:** • Assuming positions of leadership • Advancing ideas within the group • Taking a competitive stance • Managing the conversation • Influencing others' opinions	**EXPRESSED AFFECTION:** • Reassuring and supporting • Giving gifts to show appreciation • Demonstrating concern about other members personal lives • Sharing personal feelings and opinions
WANTED INCLUSION: • Frequenting heavily trafficked areas • Seeking recognition or responsibility • Getting involved in high priority projects • Going along with the majority	**WANTED CONTROL:** • Asking for help on the job • Involving others in decision-making • Requesting specific instructions or clarification • Asking for permission • Deferring to others wishes	**WANTED AFFECTION:** • Being flexible and accommodating • Listening carefully to others • Sharing feelings of anxiety • Trying to please others • Giving others more than they want/need

Available at: http://www.minahangroup.com/PDF/2004%20ODN%20Conf%20Proceedings.pdf Accessed March 29, 2006.

To ascertain your own personal needs in a group, take the Firo-B questionnaire. Consultants with credentials can administer this questionnaire to your group, or you can take it online. Most people have never tested themselves and have no idea how others would score. However, you can start to pick up clues about what kind of needs people hold by observing them. Ideally, hiring a consultant to test the group and work through the individual differences with your collaborative is the best way to identify differences and become conscious and respectful of them.

For optimal performance you need a balance of group needs in your collaborative. However, when you are inviting people to join, you have no idea what their group needs are and you may end up with an imbalance of people who need to be in. At the same time, you may have a lot of members with high inclusion needs or people who do not need or want their inclusion needs met. Having too many of one type can lead to personality conflicts. If you have a lot of people with high inclusion needs, they will spend a lot of time socializing and building group safety and may not be inclined to move ahead to the hard work of conflict and negotiation.

Some collaboratives have a number of people who talk a lot and like to argue for their point of view. I am not trying to pathologize the need for control and urge everyone with high control needs to suppress their desire to control. If you have high control needs, you may also experience a great deal of anxiety. A possible strategy is to pick and choose your fights, rather than react to everything that contradicts your beliefs. Identify which fights you need to win to make the collaborative a success. Save your energy for the important ones, and let the others go. There is a saying used by facilitators: Trust the process. To do this, let go of your need to make what you think happen and trust that through the process, something better will come to be.

When collaboratives include a number of members with high control needs, they constantly butt heads, and no one else gets a word in. As a result, the whole group becomes highly anxious, and you cannot do anything with a policy to resolve this. An offline conversation about their desire to control things may help, and open discussions of power and styles are also needed. Skilled consultants can help. The sustainability of the collaborative can be at risk if the conflict cannot be resolved to allow the group to move forward and do its work. Asking people to leave is not easy, but sometimes it is the only way the group will move forward. The group as a whole or a small leadership team might have to be entrusted with the task.

There are also cases of collaboratives where people do not have enough need to control and expect others to step up, make decisions, and do the work. This behaviour is just as maddening as the high controllers, and is just as destructive to the success of the collaborative. Sometimes avoidance of responsibility and ownership is a matter of individuals not being empowered by their home organizations so they can make decisions and share the work of the collaborative.

If you are not clear about what your home organization will let you take on, go to Chapter 3 and review how to get your organization ready to collaborate.

If you are nervous about putting out your thoughts and organizational perspectives, consider taking an assertiveness skill building course, or have the whole group participate in the training. Team building processes can also help groups of individuals learn about each other, respect the differences people bring to the group, and harness those differences and types to strengthen the group. Once you have worked through the inclusion and control stages, the last stage is easy. Trust is built. The group members have emotional capital in the bank, and they like to work with each other. This is the stage where the magic and system change happens.

Negotiation Skills
Negotiation skills will serve you well in a collaborative. When diverse groups or interests come together to decide on common goals and processes and to take action together, negotiating is fundamental to reaching agreement. Negotiating requires effective communication and joint problem-solving skills. The desire in negotiation is to create a win–win situation or, if that is not possible, to create a situation where all members can live with the decision or action taken. Partners who perceive that they have been forced to concede, or who feel that they have not been listened to, generally do not serve the collaborative well. To be effective in negotiating you must:

1. listen to the other's point of view, and use reflective and active listening;

2. not attempt to defend yourself or make threats or excuses;

3. identify the issue or problem;

4. look at options and alternatives;

5. help individuals understand the views of others;

6. break the impasse if discussions get bogged down;

7. manage conflict when it occurs;

8. help find common ground;

9. assist members to recognize agreement when it happens;

10. ensure that everyone understands the agreement.

Formalized Conflict Resolution Processes

Conflict is normal and needs to be seen as such. However, many collaboratives decide to include a formal conflict resolution process in their governance framework. This helps to park the conflict outside of the day-to-day operations and to keep the work of the collaborative moving ahead. Having a formal conflict resolution process can help prepare members for conflict by anticipating that differences will occur, and devising legitimate ground rules and processes for handling such differences when they come up. This formal process usually involves fostering communication among disputants, problem solving, and drafting agreements that meet their underlying needs.

Often a third party facilitates the process, or in some cases decides on the outcome. Some processes call for a conciliation process where one or more members of the coalition offers to serve as a go-between when differences become personal. Third party mediation is the process of referring the conflict to a time and process led by an independent mediator who is trained in dispute resolution. Third-party mediation may be necessary when conflict is significant and the stakes are high. The more parties, the more issues, and the more technically complex a dispute is, the more experienced a mediator must be to be effective (and to not make matters worse).

Tools to Manage Conflict

Rather than letting things drag on and fester, it is far better for collaborative members to become comfortable with conflict, develop the interpersonal communication tools needed to dial down the level of conflict, and use negotiation to reach agreement.

> Listening is probably the most cost effective element of a conflict management system. — Mary Rowe

The following tools can help you to manage conflict:

▶ Know yourself and be able to test your assumptions and worldviews underlying the conflict.

▶ Use active listening skills to explore the nature of the conflict:

- Get the story

- Probe/clarify meanings

- Listen for emotions

- Summarize

- Value silence

▶ Be able to identify and manage your emotions and allow others to have theirs. Use "I" statements. The DESC (Describe, Emote, Specify, Consequence) Statement provides a framework:

- **D**escribe the behaviour accurately and concisely.

- **E**xplain the impact of the behaviours on you and your organization and how you feel about it.

- **S**pecify the changes you want or ask for suggestions.

- **C**onsequences, to be explained in a positive fashion.

▶ Probe and clarify meanings. Use questions that take the speaker's understanding a step deeper, or bring out the meaning or significance of the situation for the speaker. For example, you might ask, "What is your concern about that?" or "How do you think he sees this issue?"

▶ Be able to reframe. Reframing means choosing your words carefully to:

- de-escalate hostility and calm emotions;

- move from positions to interests;

- describe issues as solvable problems; and

- develop *shared goals*, when possible, or tradeoffs.

▶ Use problem solving techniques: define the problem, explore causes, generate possible solutions, and develop criteria for a best possible solution.

▶ Negotiate solutions.

Conflict Styles

My other favourite assessment to use with collaboratives is the Thomas Killmann Conflict Mode Instrument. The TKI was developed by Kenneth W. Thomas and Ralph H. Kilmann in the early 1970s. The TKI is a self-report questionnaire designed to measure your tendencies when dealing with interpersonal conflict. It describes five different conflict-handling modes and helps you identify which of these modes you use most often. By helping you become more aware of the choices you and others make in conflict situations, the TKI and its feedback materials provide a way for you to consciously steer conflict situations in constructive directions.

Thomas and Kilmann (1974) defined five dominant orientations or modes of dealing with conflicts: avoiding, collaborating, accommodating, competing, and compromising.

Avoiding reflects inattention to the concerns of either party—a neglect, withdrawal, indifference, denial, or apathy. Avoiding as a strategy is described as, "Neutrality is maintained at all costs. Withdrawal from the situation relieves the necessity for dealing with conflict."

Collaborating is a mode with great emphasis on satisfying the concerns of all parties—to work with the other party cooperatively to find an alternative that integrates and fully satisfies the concerns of all. It requires a relatively large immediate investment in time and energy to do such joint problem solving. Collaborating as a style is, "A process used to assess several points of view and alternatives. Solutions involve consensus and diversity."

Accommodating concentrates on appeasement and trying to satisfy the other's concerns without attention to one's own concerns. There is a note of self-sacrifice in this mode, with selfless generosity, yielding to the other, and acquiescing. Accommodating is a mode which infers that "Disagreements are smoothed over so that harmony is maintained —one party gives in to another."

Competing emphasizes winning one's own concerns at the expense of another. This is a power-oriented mode, with efforts to force and dominate the other, typically in a win–lose fashion.

Compromising (sharing, or bargaining) reflects a preference for partial satisfaction of both parties' concerns. It might mean trading concessions, splitting the difference, or finding a satisfactory middle ground. Compromise, bargaining, and middle-ground positions are accepted: "Divide the pie since win–win is not possible. Win–lose would cause negative repercussions."

Adapted from Thomas, Kenneth. W., and Kilmann, Ralph. H. *Thomas-Kilmann Conflict Mode Instrument.* Xixom Incorporated.

How might you select your conflict management style?
Although you have a preferred conflict style that you fall back on automatically,

there are times when you have a choice to engage in or avoid a conflict. Consider the following six variables when confronted by a conflict.

1. HOW INVESTED ARE YOU IN THE RELATIONSHIP?

The importance of the working/personal relationship often dictates whether you will engage in a conflict. If you value the person and/or the relationship, going through the process of conflict resolution is important.

2. HOW IMPORTANT IS THE ISSUE TO YOU?

Even if the relationship is not of great value to you, you must often engage in conflict if the issue is important to you. For example, if the issue is a belief, value, or regulation that you believe in or are hired to enforce, then engaging in the conflict is necessary. If the relationship and the issue are both important to you, there is an even more compelling reason to engage in the conflict.

3. DO YOU HAVE THE ENERGY FOR THE CONFLICT?

Many say, "There is not time to do all that I want to do in a day." Often the issue is not how much time is available, but how much energy you have for what you need to do. Even in a track meet, runners are given recovery time before they have to run another race. Energy, not time, is being managed in these situations.

4. ARE YOU AWARE OF THE POTENTIAL CONSEQUENCES?

Prior to engaging in a conflict, think about anticipated consequences from engaging in the conflict. For example, there may be a risk for your safety, a risk for job loss, or an opportunity for a better working relationship. Many times people will engage in conflict and then be shocked by the outcome or consequence of engaging in the conflict. Thoughtful reflection about the consequences, both positive and negative, is useful before engaging in or avoiding a conflict.

5. ARE YOU READY FOR THE CONSEQUENCES?

After analyzing potential consequences, determine whether you are prepared for the consequences of engaging in the conflict. For example, one employee anticipated a job loss if she continued to engage in the conflict she was having with her boss over a particular issue. After careful consideration, the employee decided that she believed strongly enough about the issue to continue engaging in the conflict. Her annual contract was not renewed for the upcoming year. Because this individual had thought through the consequences of engaging in the conflict, she was prepared to be without a job for a while and was able to plan for this outcome financially and emotionally.

6. WHAT ARE THE CONSEQUENCES IF YOU DO NOT ENGAGE IN THE CONFLICT?

To avoid losing a sense of self, there are times when you must engage in conflict. Most people have core values, ideas, beliefs, or morals. If individuals are going to sacrifice one of their core beliefs by avoiding conflict, personal loss of respect must be considered. In such cases, even if they are not excited about confronting the conflict, they must carefully consider the consequences of evading the conflict. When the personal consequences of turning away from the conflict outweigh all other factors, then a person usually must take part in the conflict.

Modified from the *Foundation Coalition*, July 20, 2006, at http://www. foundationcoalition.org/home/keycomponents/teams/conflict1f.html.

Summary

Conflict is normal. To normalize conflict you have to talk about it. When conflict is rooted in power, your collaborative needs to explore people's sources of power and explore the assumptions behind these perceptions. I am always astounded at how few people are in touch with their own power, even when they have statutory authority under legislation. Wanting and needing inclusion, control, and affection is part of normal group processes. As a leader, it helps to see that resistance and conflict are gifts. If you can create a safe space for truth telling, the issues can emerge to be dealt with, rather than left underground to fester and emerge later in the process when the stakes are higher.

There are many tools available to deal with power issues and conflict in groups, including developing your own personal capacity to be comfortable with conflict situations, and allowing for the emotions and perceptions to be shared rather than shutting down the conversation. Interpersonal communication tools like Active Listening and Describe, Emote, Specify and Consequence statements support effective dialogue, and negotiation skills can build the agreement to resolve the conflict issues. A policy-making focus helps to organize and channel the conflict. If the situation warrants it, collaboratives can also build formal conflict resolution processes into their terms of reference and collaborative agreements.

CHAPTER 13:
Leadership

The most dangerous leadership myth is that leaders are born—that there is a genetic factor to leadership. This myth asserts that people simply either have certain charismatic qualities or not. That's nonsense; in fact, the opposite is true. Leaders are made rather than born. —Warren G. Bennis

This chapter explores what leadership needs to look like in a collaborative structure. Keep in mind that the leadership challenges of the three basic trans-organization structures—hierarchical, democratic, and laissez-faire—are different and the type of leadership must be applied according to its unique needs and situation. However, when the collaborative aspires to a power sharing model, an affiliative form of leadership is appropriate. The chapter also discusses what is meant by lateral leadership, defines its characteristics, presents tips and tools on how to become more of a lateral leader, and explores how to build an organizational learning culture. Most importantly, the chapter discusses how to develop the personal attributes of self-awareness and letting go of control that contribute to accountability and trust building in a healthy, high functioning collaborative.

Leadership in the 21st century is a vague and ambiguous term. Previous generations defined leadership by associating it with those people who held titles and authority and wielded their power to achieve particular ends. Politicians, soldiers, and corporate bosses all wore the leadership label. They were leaders in a hierarchical organization and usually part of the management and decision-making structure in some way.

This notion started to change sometime late in the 20th century. We still valued the leaders in traditional hierarchy, but the notion of leadership broadened to include non-traditional forms of leadership, often those functions that take on a more feminine form—nurturing, coaching, and building participation. Female leaders worked to bring peace to Northern Ireland, and experimented with different forms of leadership in social movements including the Civil Rights and Feminist movements. Gro Harlem Brundtland, the prime minister of Norway, convened a global process under the credentials of the United Nations. This body, the World Commission on Environment and Development, examined the planet's critical environment and development problems and formulated realistic proposals to solve them, to create a global agenda for change. The report *Our Common Future* (1987) was the first global action plan for taking care of the planet. I remember reading it and using it as a primer for my political work.

Because of Brundland's paradigm-changing work, the motto of change agents became *think global and act local*. Grassroots activists mobilized people to adopt local recycling programs, advocate for bike lanes, and improve public transit. The complexity of the environmental mess was such that saving the planet needed dispersed leadership. It needed just about everyone owning the power they had over their decisions and choices to change their lifestyle, as well as the policy changes at the top. Leadership needed to emerge on an individual basis along with groups and governments. All of a sudden there was a need for just about everyone to exhibit leadership, to own power, and to model behaviour change.

Leadership began to be seen as something that anyone could exhibit, rather than just those in traditional leadership roles. Not to under-emphasize all the leadership development that went on in the adult education, labour, and social movements throughout the 20th century, but the Bruntland report was unique in its scale. Here was a prime minister who did not hold the authority to define a problem for the entire globe; her jurisdictional power was limited to her nation state. The United Nation's jurisdiction in this area was negligible, although it gave the process some legitimacy. Yet all these limitations did not deter her and the commission from urging all nation states and their peoples to action. She felt she could make a difference, she laid out a plan, and she urged others around the entire planet to do the same.

By the late 20th century, many people bought into the notion that leadership was not just something exhibited by those with power or authority, but was rather an activity of "mobilizing people to tackle tough problems" (Heifetz, 1994). Leadership began to be equated with making changes. And these new forms of leadership began to be described and characterized as shared, feminine, empowered, and grassroots leadership. One characteristic of this new form of leadership was that it was not done just by those who held formal titles and who had employees to order around, but was done by ordinary people in groups. The groups could be the local sport associations or a national advocacy organization, and leadership could be more democratic than what people experienced in the workplace.

> Leadership can be explored as a social process - something that happens between people. It is not so much what leaders do, as something that arises out of social relationships. As such it does not depend on one person, but on how people act together to make sense of the situations that face them. (Doyle & Smith, 2005)

The origins of leadership for collaboration emerged from these new forms of leadership without authority. Author David Crislip describes leadership in collaboratives as "leading as a peer, not a superior." This type of leadership emerged in grassroots organizations all over the world. But as we learned in Chapter 4, not all collaboratives are organized alike and different leadership styles and competencies may be required for different types of organizations. The trans-organizational structure might be the biggest factor that determines the style of leadership needed in a collaborative.

Leadership Challenges of Three Basic Trans-Organization Structures

Trans-organization systems (TS) is a technical term used to describe supra-systems that consist of separate autonomous organizations spanning organizational boundaries. A TS functions as more than the sum of its separate constituents by enabling decision-making and task-performance on behalf of member groups, who retain autonomous identities and goals (for example, alliances, coalitions, partnerships, and joint ventures). As mentioned in Chapter 1, the term collaborative has evolved over the last decade to describe this type of supra-organizational structure.

Hierarchical Trans-Organizational Structure:

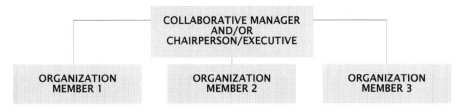

This hierarchical structure is most aligned with traditional competencies of leadership, such as vision setting, providing direction, and communicating. The structure reflects the belief that a leader at the top is essential. The task of the leader is to define the destination, develop the blueprint to get there, and hold people accountable through measurements and reward. The leader's work is to bring others on board, enroll others into the process, align the activities and goals, and inspire everyone to complete their assigned tasks.

The challenge with this form of leadership is that since the leader is so powerful and capable, followers may lapse into passivity; if somebody is on top, then somebody must be on the bottom. If there is any kind of participation, it takes place as consultation by the leader and input by the followers. And in this situation, the leadership usually lacks the coercive power that comes with the executive role in a corporate or government hierarchy, which motivates people do their assigned tasks or else they risk losing their jobs. In a collaborative, where everyone is there voluntarily, fear is not a good motivator. Therefore, a traditional leader in a collaborative lacks the energy (coercive power and fear) to make things happen. Lacking coercive power, the leader in a hierarchical collaborative has to rely on other things to motivate people, including clear appeals to self-interest, charm, and charisma (communication and selling skills); a powerful vision; and effective coordination (project manager skills).

Democratic TS Structure

In this structure, much of the leadership challenge comes from unspoken assumptions people hold about their ideals of what a democratic organization should look like. They may not have much experience with one—they rarely exist—however, we live in so-called democratic societies with associated platitudes and ideals, some from as far back as Athenian democracy in 500 BC. Democratic organizing options include issues such as the one person–one vote rule. The group might struggle with the issue of striving for consensus rather than majority rules and the meaning of consensus (do we need total unanimity?). Other questions include:

• Are we a representative or a participative democratic organization?

• Do we need a constituent base to be truly accountable or are our member organizations enough for accountability for our change strategies?

A democratic organization needs participative processes to develop a vision and for governance, especially decision-making, trust building, and the coordination work amongst multiple partners. These processes can facilitate the egalitarian leadership and commitment needed amongst disparate and autonomous partners to co-create a new mission and collaborative organization. This type of organization needs to develop its governance framework because the decision-making method and policies provide the structural framework for members to exercise shared power. This requires an upfront investment in discussion-based processes to reach agreement. Leaders not comfortable with process, who are untrained to lead consensus building, will find it difficult to let go of their task focus and allow the creation of a democratic organization. It requires skill to facilitate and build consensus and move a group forward while in a peer role. Many people feel they come to this role naturally, but training in facilitation skills and a commitment to letting go of a personal need to control is critical for leadership in a democratic TS. Time and time again, developing collaboratives become so tolerant of staying stuck that instead of developing a minimal amount of structure (including a vision for focus), they go round and round trying to figure out what they came together to do.

Other pitfalls of democratic TSs that rely on consensus decision-making is something facilitators call the tyranny of the minority. Consensus decision-making is not voting unanimously or in unanimity, needing everyone to agree to the action, but there is a component which allows group members to block the process. This permits one or a few people to disrupt the decision-making process and stop the group from making any decision. By doing so, members take a highly ethical stance or they engage in a political power play to ensure their agenda wins the day. Discerning between the two intentions is not easy and will sorely test the leadership and group.

Self-Organizing Network Structure

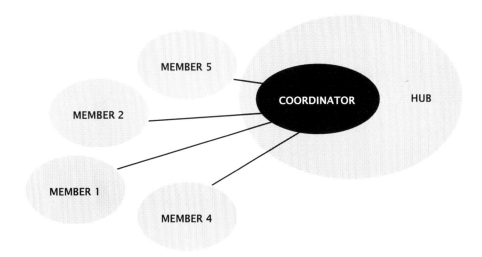

The form of leadership associated with what Margaret Wheatley and others describe as self-organizing systems or complex adaptive systems uses less control. They make the argument that the problem set or mess may look highly chaotic, but there are underlying patterns that, once they emerge, will focus the connections and permit a strategy to unfold.

This school of thought makes the argument that collaboratives should stay in the unorganized space to wait for the natural order to emerge, rather than applying some external model just to make sense out of the chaos. This form of collaboration is more of a network than a TS, as there is no common purpose or transformation of knowledge. Another way of looking at it is that the group is in the early stages of system development or may choose not to organize with a common purpose that transforms knowledge. Instead, it shares knowledge as in a learning community or community of practice. Everyone belongs for their own individual learning and many may never want to work together to make something happen externally. There is nothing wrong with these reasons to connect with others; it is just not a change strategy focused on a complex issue in a shared external environment.

Sometimes just the action of convening a group and hosting a dialogue can foster the development of a network. People then keep in touch and take action individually. This network can have a great deal of influence in terms of advocacy and policy change. The challenge, however, is that there is no control at the centre.

If you have pulled together a network for advocacy purposes, and if people have not signed on to support a common agenda, they very well may use your issue to advocate for their pet project or preferred solution. Who is going to stop them or even know what they are up to? In my experience, this is about making sure people do desired actions like call their political representative. In these networks with no accountability mechanism in place, people often feel like they do not have to take action since no one is going to follow up!

The leadership style becoming associated with this form of collaboration is labelled invisible, transformational, or authentic leadership. The art of convening is the competency most associated with this form of leadership. Convening involves pulling people together to explore if there is the energy and desire to work together. It includes hosting a dialogue about a topic with or without visible recognition and withholding one's opinion, not engaging in a selling process, and allowing others to take the space for opinions. The leadership skill involves holding space for the dialogue to happen. It requires highly-developed facilitation skills and enough self-awareness to put one's ego away and let whatever the group wants to happen, happen. The group members own and take the power to work together, or they do not. This leadership style is mostly about letting go of control, and is the total opposite of hierarchical leadership.

Lateral Leadership:
Because of their potential for power sharing, collaboratives and self-organizing systems are a different kind of organization than workplaces. In our society, employees and managers know best how to behave in hierarchical organizations, where the boss is often treated as a supreme ruler because of the coercive power, formal authority, and ability to reward or reprimand that come with the position. But in a collaborative, formed on a voluntary basis, where no one has coercive power, and when everyone around the table is a volunteer, traditional leadership skills such as providing direction and communicating expectations simply alienates others. Participating and leading in a collaborative require different skills and leadership approaches. This is not always apparent to all members, and unless there is open and honest communication about leadership and participation expectations, most people revert to what they know.

What are the characteristics of lateral leadership?
Lateral leadership occurs when you do not have the coercive power that is attached to a position of power in a hierarchical structure. Anyone with or without a title at any time can provide this kind of leadership. The power sourced with this kind of leadership is usually informal, such as the power to influence and

persuade and the ability to network. You need to be able to communicate and convince, without having coercive power, as every participant is free to exercise the power to walk. Many of the skills of lateral leadership are synonymous with adult learning principles, and many skills are associated with organizational development or change management. Some of these skills include influencing and persuading, critical thinking, effective questioning, and decision-making. This form of leadership requires a great deal of self-awareness and emotional intelligence so that the individual leader's needs are taken care of (by him or herself) and the lateral leader can focus on the needs of others.

How does one become more of a lateral leader?
If you are needy or demanding of others, they will not work with you in a voluntary capacity. In the cross-boundary world of collaboration, the mutual benefit of working together is gradually explored to build trust. An autocratic approach based on the use of coercive power does not work because it is a one-sided transaction. If you come with a one-track advocacy message or a strong position, these will get lost in the group's desire to meet mutual needs. If genuine change is to take place, leaders have to change themselves, give up their status as leaders and experts, and listen for the group's wisdom to emerge.

In all the new approaches, leaders start with themselves by managing their stress, discovering and meeting their own needs, refining their emotional intelligence, and using themselves as a finely tuned instrument to catalyze people to make change. This journey of personal discovery cannot be undertaken alone or with biblio-therapy (reading). The journey needs experiences you can only get through transformational leadership programs, coaching, and psychotherapy where you can get feedback and do the hard work of personal growth. While working on yourself on the inside, outwardly you can put into practice lateral leadership processes to bridge diverse cultures, undertake learning across organizational boundaries, and reveal and challenge assumptions that limit thinking and action. Here are some tips on how to incorporate lateral leadership into your collaborative processes.

Build a Learning Culture:
Everyone in a collaborative needs to learn from each other for something new to emerge, whether a plan, a new program, or a service. But in many places, including the NPO sector, it is not acceptable to admit that you lack a skill or knowledge; it is much safer to take few risks and keep quiet to prevent others from finding out your secret. If everyone takes this same attitude, however, nothing will change. For learning to take place you need to acknowledge that you do not

know everything about a lot of things. You need to model that there are no silly questions so you can create a climate of openness and honesty and permit people to just be how they are, warts and all. You must model a willingness to learn and experiment. Of course, many of us have issues about being imperfect, which is why I urge a journey of self-discovery so you can give up self-defeating beliefs like the need to be perfect.

Learning is the most critical process that stimulates the acceptance of others. To reach agreement and make decisions together, a dialogue has to take place where people can be honest and open about their self-interest and needs. If you can create a climate of learning, then the common purpose and vision can emerge through dialogue and negotiation. Everyone in a multi-organizational collaborative experiences some form of culture shock and culture clash. Culture is a belief system—organizations and sectors all have many covert beliefs that only come to the surface when you work with people from outside your group. Learning about each other helps to create a foundation for a new culture to emerge, taking the best from each organization of origin.

Accountability:
Accountability is a trendy buzz word, often used disparagingly toward people in government or the NPO sector by people not enamoured of government spending to alleviate social problems. In many office settings, the term accountability is frequently used to assign blame. This widespread behaviour leads us to assume that if we can avoid being responsible, then we cannot be held to account. This kind of thinking leads to avoidance of responsibilities and poor follow-through. Instead, Paula Martin in *A New Kind Of Accountability,* says:

> a more effective approach to accountability is to use it for prevention, not punishment. The question you should be asking members is, "Who is accountable to make sure this outcome happens as planned?" The accountable person's job is to do whatever is possible in order to assure the defined outcome is achieved. If something goes wrong, the question to ask is, "What can we learn from this so we can do a better job next time?"

Martin goes on to say that accountability has to be voluntarily accepted, and the best way to accomplish that is through team participation. Participative processes can be used not only to develop the vision, but are especially useful for decision-making, trust building, and the coordination work amongst multiple partners. Change management tools from organization development and adult education can facilitate the egalitarian leadership and commitment needed to build a culture of participation and accountability.

Truly shared leadership takes place when the problem is owned by everyone and all members create the plan and share responsibility for implementing it. In the end, it is a better plan because the ideas in the plan are everyone's and everyone becomes committed to it. The plan will better reflect the energy and capacity of the members as well. Since the plan is seen by all as doable, the group will feel accountable for it and assume the responsibility for making it happen. See Appendix F for a model to help you assign responsibility and ensure communication with stakeholders during project implementation.

Trust:
Trust is more of a feeling than a fact or objective concept, but it is the undercurrent to all relationship transactions. Without trust, people are not going to take action. This can be seen in simple day-to-day traffic management. If the people in your community did not respect red lights or stop signs, it would be hard to drive through a green light. When we trust that our neighbours will obey traffic lights and signs, we willingly follow the rules, trusting that everyone else does too.

The same holds true for a collaborative. People will sit around in early meetings trying to determine what they can trust and put their faith into. If you are convening the meeting, they will be looking to determine whether to trust you first and foremost. You need to begin with the trust in yourself that everything will work out the way it needs to. To encourage this kind of trust in the unknown, sometimes we say things like *trust the process*, or *trust the group*. You have to believe it first before others will. You have to give up the need to control and trust that the group will come up with something far better than anyone could alone.

Secondly, you must be trustworthy. This behaviour entails exhibiting openness by disclosing what you are thinking and feeling. If you make a statement, elaborate why you think that way and your feelings. This permits others to be open too. Most importantly, follow through on your commitments so people can trust that your words are aligned with your actions. There are lots of good talkers, but you cannot build trust with talk alone. In addition, create conditions to trust. Ensure there is transparency around decision-making. If decisions are being made between meetings and that is contrary to your policy, share with the group what happened and why. If you have no policy on decision-making, get the group to make one as soon as possible.

Hold people accountable for their promises. Ask gently if they have been able to do what they promised, and if not, when it will get done. Ask if there are obstacles, and ask the group to come up with strategies to overcome the obstacles. There is nothing more frustrating to those who follow through on their commitments than to see others who do not are left off the hook. In addition, make sure the groups objectives are clear and if there is a collective vision, use that to bring people back when the discussion goes off track. And finally, share the rewards and the recognition. In a collaborative (really, any group effort) things happen because of the joint effort of all involved. Put your ego on the back burner and stroke others, over and over. It is all about them, not you. They will trust you because you get that simple fact.

Explore:
This issue is so important that a chapter is devoted to it (see Chapter 5). Change happens rapidly; by the time you have a common vision and strategy developed for the collaborative, the external environment may have changed drastically and you are forced to modify your original plans. Somebody has to pay attention to these trends and external events to see them coming and bring them to the attention of the collaborative. Environmental scanning involves curiosity and paying attention to the information in the external environment. You get information by listening to news broadcasts and reading newspapers, magazines, and broadcast emails. This is the work of the manager/executive director and everyone who works in a professional role.

Paying attention to the external environment is the critical boundary spanning function for those in senior positions. If you leave your office and represent your organization in a collaborative, this is what you are doing. Be sure to take what you learn and notice back home so that your organization or TS can monitor and keep track of changes, analyze trends, and identify ways to respond to changing circumstances. While many wallow in a state of having too much information, the explorer surveying uncharted complex systems looks for patterns to give meaning to all the unorganized information. Pattern recognition is a highly developed art for social change agents, and is the result of formal and informal education. A traditional liberal arts education can form the basis for this competency and can be augmented by continuous reading of newspapers and the latest books in business and politics. You can cheat with book summaries and seminars; however, whatever grabs your attention deserves in-depth study.

Most important is a basic knowledge of history. All of our current issues are rooted in historical circumstance. Government and the non-profit sector are organized the way they are because of decisions taken by our forebears and previous governments. One of the most complex issues the NPO sector faces is the low wage structure. Because of low wages, young people are not coming into the sector or remaining in underpaid positions. However, without an understanding of how this situation came about and why, NPO problem solving efforts will lead to superficial solutions that will not last. History matters! Ask why and seek answers. You must also heed the short history of collaborations and learn from previous efforts. We are pioneers in developing this form of organization structure, but as the pioneers did, we need to learn from each other and those who came before to discover what works or what does not when trying to create a new collaboration. Many collaborative members believe that collaboration is a simple process and that few skills are needed, even when presented with the statistics of high failure rates. History says otherwise.

Build relationships by attending to people and processes. The primary way to prepare for the unknown is to attend to the quality of your relationships, to how well you know and trust one another. The research is clear that in every emergency situation, the outcome is much better when the players have pre-developed relationships. An emergency or crisis is not the time to build relationships. Think of the collective relationships of your collaborative as an emotional capital account. The more you have invested in them, the more you can take out of the account. This is a great asset when adversity strikes or conflict erupts. If you have little in your emotional capital account, then it is easy for people to cut their losses and walk away. Build your emotional capital through opportunities to get to know each other by holding social events and retreats, and by developing shared projects. Even in regular meetings, make sure there is time for networking. Have refreshments ready before the meeting as well as during breaks. Use participative processes that engage people in discussion, not debate.

In the absence of empirical research on the NPO sector, IASCP researcher Tom Zizys looked at collaboration in the for-profit sector. He found that poor relationship building among organizations led to failure in their collaborative efforts. Relationships are built over time, and time and energy for relationship building must be allocated. Although mission driven instead of profit driven, these findings provide guidance for the NPO sector which, in my experience, can be just as task-orientated and neglectful of relationships amongst its own staff and collaborative members.

Awareness:
To work in this paradigm, collaborators have to pay attention to their own development and contribution to the group. The approach is sometimes called *self as instrument*. This term describes an awareness of how you bring yourself to groups, such as your assumptions and theories of how people work in groups, the ability to observe yourself in a group, and the ability to create healthy group processes by using your own personal needs and emotions as tools. The thinking

goes that if you can be comfortable with your own anxiety and fear, then you can allow others their anxiety and fears without having to fix them. This is not easy when our culture encourages us not to feel, or to buy something if we feel out of sorts. These skills are fostered under the skill development banner of emotional intelligence. Getting comfortable with fear and anxiety allows you to live with the ambiguity of complex problems. If you can manage your own fears well enough to ride the waves of change, you can keep your head when everyone else is losing theirs, as the saying goes.

You can discover so much about your own personal psychology. It takes a journey to uncover the mystery of ourselves and to develop the compassion for ourselves that we need before we can truly feel compassionate for others. Individuals who have a deep understanding of themselves are able to live authentically with no need for projecting their fears or doubts onto others.

Let Go of Control:
Pick and choose your fights is the true underlying message that chaos theorists give when they say there are too many variables to try and control. People are knocking themselves out trying to manage the unmanageable. Instead, think of your environment as three concentric circles (see Figure 18). The inner circle represents all that you can control. The middle circle represents all that you can influence but not control. The outer circle represents those people, events, circumstances, etc. that you can neither influence nor control.

Figure 18: Model of Your Environment

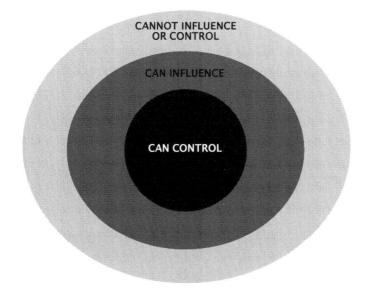

Spend time and focus energy on the two inner circles because that is where you can have an impact. In the outer circle, you are wasting energy on things you can or will have little effect upon. Do not spend your time trying to increase your span of control; leverage your influence instead. Accept that if you are a leader, some people will get angry with you, and that you will be an easy target for some people's problems. To others, you may represent a system that they feel is wrong. You are not the target. People make themselves angry—you cannot. They make sense out of what happens to them. You can only take responsibility for what you do.

Discernment is the activity of figuring out what you can control and what you cannot control. Once you own what you are personally responsible for, you can see the span over which you really have total control is very, very small. Use your energy and smarts to discover where the leverage points in the complexity are and where you may not control the situation. Perhaps by taking small actions you can shift the course of events. Paradoxically, letting go of control helps you to develop systemic thinking skills. You begin to see the interconnections in complex situations and the interpersonal dynamics that lead to stalemate. Realize that the courage to shift the dynamic through a well-timed conversation might be what is required to change the course of events, rather than giving up or developing a high level power play. You begin to experience less stress, and you feel much lighter knowing most everything is really out of your span of control.

Summary
To conclude, leadership in a collaborative is very complex work and requires a great deal of personal development, self awareness, and high-level systems thinking skills. Leading in a collaborative is much different than managing in the workplace, where the traditional leadership skills of delegating and providing direction are backed up with coercive power. Instead, a new approach to leadership is required that is more about sharing power than exerting it, one that includes members in decision-making, and that co-creates a new future that works for everyone. The lateral leader must foster persistence, energy, and passion to motivate and bring the process to where it needs to go. These qualities are the result of living a balanced and joyful life. They do not come from work alone; you must source them outside of the work so that you bring them with you.

CHAPTER 14:
Conclusion

I would not give a fig for the simplicity on this side of complexity. But I would give my life for the simplicity on the other side.—Oliver Wendell Holmes

As we moved toward the 21st century, a revolutionary process improvement emerged at the grassroots level of business and government service delivery: the joining together of organizations. When two or more organizations come together for shared service delivery, back office support, or to work together to change policy, they need to create a new hybrid structure to support joint activities. As practitioners started using collaboratives for social change, they discovered that collaboratives are complex organizational structures that are not easy to develop or maintain. In particular, they are fraught with conflict and power issues, and require a systematic colloborative governance framework. This book was developed to meet that need.

Governance is a Function

The key message in this book is that governance is a function. A collaborative does not need a board of directors to undertake this function, unlike traditional stand-alone organizations. Instead, leaders must assume the functions of governance. The governance responsibilities of a collaborative's steering committee/body can be organized under three functional areas: representing the community, providing leadership, and monitoring and evaluation.

The work of governance, such as decision-making, securing resources, strategic planning, and policy-making, use and consolidate power and

197

therefore are prone to lead to conflict. Because these issues are the most likely causes of failure, practitioners need to be aware of governance issues throughout the development process and build the appropriate governance structure on as-needed basis.

Accountability Adds to the Complexity

Not only are collaboratives accountable to the broader community and to funders, as with any non-profit, they are also accountable to the member agencies. This additional level of accountability is often overlooked. Individual members may or may not be empowered to make decisions on their agency's behalf. Key decisions about strategic direction, resource allocation, and funding are usually high-risk decisions for individual members. When individual members lack clear boundaries for their decision-making role, they may be likely to avoid taking on responsibility and fully participating.

Get Your own House in Order!

The first step to developing successful collaboratives is to get your own organizational house in order. Prior to even getting involved in any collaborations, organizations need to develop their own in-house organizational policy on participating in collaboratives. The purpose of this policy is to clearly identify the organizational objectives for engaging in collaborations and the criteria for decision-making. The policy also provides guidance to staff on their role and the expectations surrounding their participation in external collaborations. Chapter 3 provided an in-depth discussion and framework for developing an organizational collaboration policy.

Develop Collaborations Thoughtfully and Systematically

This book laid out a six-step model for developing successful collaborations, exploring in-depth the governance structure required at each step in the process. As governance is the solution to issues dealing with power and conflict, each step of the process requires the convener, initiator, or leadership to put in place the appropriate and minimalist governance needed to move the process forward. The step-by-step model does not require you to stop the initial momentum to put a detailed governance structure in place like that found in an established organization. Instead, it suggests just enough structure to facilitate the work at each step.

Step 1 Determine the Need for a Collaborative and Explore the Problem Set

This step begins the process of looking outside an organization's boundaries for additional resources and knowledge to scope out a complex problem. The process can begin with one person deciding to seek external help. Additional participants can be invited in at this stage, but Steps 1 and 2 are usually undertaken by an individual, sole agency, or committee. As these steps focus on data gathering and determining the feasibility of taking on a collaborative approach, they may need little in the way of governance—one person or organization is often making all the decisions. Step 1 begins the process of scoping out the complexity of the problem using tools such as literature reviews and environmental scans.

Step 2 Motivation to Act

At this step, the convener first becomes aware of power dynamics and the potential for conflict between potential members and stakeholders. Mapping the environment and scoping the problem are fraught with power dynamics and potential conflicts with possible members. Becoming aware of the motivation of system actors and identifying possible political dynamics will permit more strategic decisions around member selection and identifying knowledge resources in Step 3 of the framework. Steps 1 and 2 comprise the feasibility stage of the development process.

Step 3 Who should belong?

The decisions about who gets to play in the sandbox are fraught with political danger. Invite everyone and you attract those with agendas, but little in the way of resources. Invite a select few and you set yourself up for criticism by those shut out. It is a no-win situation, so you need to be transparent and openly identify your criteria for member selection for public scrutiny. Member selection criteria and an initial decision-making process are critical to start off the collaboration governance structure in Step 3.

Step 4 Collaborative Planning—Exploring common ground and committing to work together

The next step is critical for any self-organizing process that is co-created by its members. The task is to reach agreement on the common vision and strategy to address the problem set. In this step, participants agree to define the problem and put boundaries around the parts that the collaborative can address. Collecting data and analyzing possible approaches and solutions to prepare an intervention become the next tasks. While participants reach agreement on the problem set and possible solutions, the natural conflicts amongst members surface and get put on the table. At this step, a skilled facilitator can guide the conversation and decision-making to ensure covert issues see the light of day. The group can then normalize the conflicts and build the commitment to the desired future they imagine together.

Step 5 Building an Organization: A mechanism to implement the plan
This is the most intense step where you build a governance structure to suit the plan. If a collaborative has come through Step 4 and overcome the conflict and power dynamics of working across organizational borders to determine an intervention strategy or plan, then the implementation of that plan becomes the work of this stage.

At this step you assemble the resources to make the plan a reality. You also need a governance structure to manage those human and financial resources that you secure to implement the plan. Policy-making becomes the primary governance tool to deal with repetitive and reoccurring situations, like spending and saving money, hiring staff and consultants, and who reports to whom. You may not need all the policies of an established organization, but depending on the work involved in your intervention (as with architecture, form follows function), you need a policy framework to ensure meetings happen, communication takes place, and procedures are established to support the day-to-day work. Many collaboratives opt to adopt the policy framework of their lead or trustee agency to avoid the work of reinventing the policy wheel. Keep in mind the nature of the work: some collaboratives focus on social marketing initiatives and need sophisticated communications policies that many non-profits do not need or have in place. Customize the governance framework to the situation.

Step 6 Evaluation: Is the collaborative doing its work effectively?
The last step in the model is the evaluation step. More and more collaboratives are reaching this step, but the academic literature is still sparse. There is little evidence that interventions undertaken by collaboratives are more effective than those undertaken by sole providers. The literature, both academic and grey, contains mainly descriptive case studies with a focus on process learnings as opposed to the content of the intervention. Chapter 10 includes a tool to undertake a process evaluation. As the field matures, the focus on learning about process may lessen and the focus on intervention content should rise in priority. You need to know if the investment in collaborative capacity building is worth it.

This book provided an in-depth look at how to incorporate governance into the six-step development framework laid out in *Alliances, Coalitions and Partnerships: Building Collaborative Organizations*. Although a governance structure is critical to help the collaborative move through power and conflict issues, the other two streams in the model of organizational effectiveness — trust building and work coordination processes — are just as important to ensure the collaborative comes together to work effectively.

Fostering Collaboration Quickly

The chapter on rapid development of collaboratives presents a process plan that a facilitator can use when a new group comes together in a high-risk situation. The process plan assumes that the group members do not know each other and must therefore move through the stages of group development. The process plan, although highly concentrated and designed to have the group problem solve as quickly as possible, can be slowed down to accommodate a less rushed situation. It can also be modified to include a standalone visioning and planning process. The key learning from this chapter is that all groups must move through the stages of group development. Take active steps to help build group trust and lower anxiety so the group can gel and perform.

Managing Conflict and Political Dynamics in Collaboratives

Readers of my first book and participants in my training sessions are always most interested in conflict and politics. It is the source of most dysfunction in collaborative as well as in sole organizations. Politics is a dirty word for many, and conflict is something to be avoided at all costs. There are not many real-life examples where politics and conflict are handled really well. People who work in the political arena probably have the highest comfort level with conflict and politics, as most of their work is consumed with it. What the public rarely sees is how much of the conflict in the political workplace is managed very well without rancour and raging debate. Some estimate that 95% of all the matters before a council or legislature pass without major debate and public controversy.

There are many avenues within government to resolve conflict. Assembling all the perspectives is expected at the bureaucratic level and happens with a more political lens at the committee level of government. What the public rarely sees is how members of different parties listen to each and amend their proposals to accommodate differing points of view to get something to the next approval level. Because controversy attracts viewers and sells newspapers, the public rarely sees the cooperation and give-and-take that happens much of the time. Instead, people see the disagreements and shouting, get turned off, and silently resolve never to be like those idiots they see on TV.

My key message is that collaboration exists because there is unresolved conflict somewhere in the area where your complex problem resides. Only by embracing the attitude espoused by some political players who express their enthusiasm for a good fight by grunting "Bring it on" will the unsolvable be solved. By raising your own comfort level with conflict, allowing the conflict to be what it needs to be, and using governance tools to manage political dynamics and conflicts, will you find that magic happens and breakthroughs are made.

Leadership: Different types required for different structures
In my first book I described the leadership traits needed to work across boundaries, called *lateral leadership*. I was describing a new kind of leadership that is variously called facilitative leadership or invisible leadership. All of these new forms of leadership are required in a democratic or self-organizing form of organization and governance. I also acknowledge that some collaboratives are not run democratically and their members might be comfortable with a more traditional type of leadership associated with hierarchical forms of organization and governance.

Democratic governance and lateral leadership styles take more time and energy than hierarchy styles. They may be perfectly acceptable in situations where there is little coming together in real time for face-to-face interaction (e.g., in geographically dispersed collaborations). In addition, they can be used in high trust advocacy collaborations where the objectives are clear and members are highly trusting of a small team to undertake strategy formation and implementation.

Again, form follows function—depending on the structure needed for your work, your choice of leadership style is dependent on the genotype underlying your organization and governance structure.

Is the future of collaboration a virtual one?
As I am writing this book, I am inundated with workshops, films, and newspaper articles on the new world that will be open up via Virtual Collaboration and Web 2.0. Virtual Collaboration presents an opportunity for improved productivity, say the technocratic experts. New technical platforms

for Web meetings are announced every day. Webinars are supposed to allow worldwide participation in conferences and learning/working events.

My experience is that unless the technology is top-notch, where everyone has expensive video conferencing technology, we are not there yet. Most webinars are still audio teleconferencing with a Website or PowerPoint presentation. This methodology can be quite good if a trained leader runs the event, but most meeting leaders are unable to manage a meeting in real time, let alone in the virtual world. Again, it is a matter of training and meeting structure. Any event needs to be treated as a developing group in evolution using the stages of group development. Whether the collaboration is face-to-face or virtual, meetings need to be structured and governance tools put in place. Trust needs to be consciously built in any collaboration.

If a collaboration is going to operate virtually most of the time, pay attention to how you and all the members will build trust, manage the work, and deal with power and conflict. A governance structure that holds people accountable for their promises and pays attention to group process will go a long way in helping your collaboration build trust, even in cyberspace.

Final Thoughts on the Future of Collaboration
My hope is that the key message from my first book—the importance of people processes—did not get lost in this one. Almost every research study on collaboration stresses the importance of good group processes as a precondition for organizational success. My first book emphasized that message, and I hope that it came through here, even though this book is focused on governance processes.

The other process stream I identified in the first book was work coordination. This area can be better identified as project management. Many books and courses focus on imparting the skills of project management. As collaborations undertake complex interventions involving many different projects and programs, managers require sophisticated project manager skills. Thousands of courses are available. If you do not have project management skills, make it a top priority for your professional development.

Funders are encouraging more collaboration at the grassroots level in spite of a lack of evidence of their value in many areas. Collaborative processes need solid academic research to establish their value as we will turn more and more to this organizational form to help deal with the complexity of the issues government and the non-profit system face. A complex organization goes hand-in-hand in with solving a complex problem. Collaboratives are the best tool we have at present to change large systems. However, we must use them judiciously so they are not discarded as last year's latest and greatest, but instead become a widespread process innovation that helps us overcome stagnant and stalemated large systems. Those large systems need to be responsive and pro-active so they achieve our greatest hopes and aspirations for the collective good.

I wrote this book because I continue to observe that collaboratives are not paying enough attention to the governance piece of collaborative capacity building. Yet many experience conflicts that stymie the innovative interventions and results required to deal with complex social messes. The IASC project discovered that almost all of the collaborations in the local NPO sector remain informal and unstructured. It is my hope that by providing this guide on how to build a governance structure, collaboratives will move forward in their pioneering work of addressing society's most pressing complex problems.

Bibliography

Ackoff, R. L. (1981). *Creating the corporate future*. John Wiley and Sons.

Armstrong, J. (1998). *Learning Partnerships: A Review of IDRC Secretariats Literature Review*, Volume 2.

Block, P. (1989). *The empowered manager: Positive political skills at work.* Jossey Bass.

Bradshaw, P. (2002). Reframing board-staff relations: Exploring the governance function using a storytelling metaphor. *Nonprofit Management and Leadership*, 12(4), 471-484.

Bradshaw, P., Hayday, B., Armstrong, R. L., & Johanne Rykert, L. (1998). Nonprofit governance models: Problems and prospects. Paper presented at the ARNOVA Conference, Seattle Washington. Retrieved from http://www.buildingmovement.org/artman/uploads/nonprofit_governance_models.pdf.

Butterfoss, F. D. & Francisco, V. T. (2004). Evaluating community partnerships and coalitions with practitioners in mind. *Health Promotion Practice*, 5(2), 108-114.

Chrislip D. D. (2004). Collaborative leadership and community health governance.Retrieved April 2009 from http://www.skillfulmeans.org/stories/Chrislip_CommHealthGov.pdf

Comfort, A. J. & Weiner, B. M. (1998). Governance in public-private community health partnerships: A survey of the community care network demonstration sites. *Nonprofit Management & Leadership*, 8(4), 311-332.

Cook, J. & Renz, D. (1998–2000). *Comprehensive abstracted bibliography of papers and journal articles on nonprofit boards and governance.* Midwest Center for Nonprofit Leadership, University of Missouri, Kansas City. Retrieved from http://mwcnl.bsbpa.umkc.edu/research/RESEARCH.HTM

Cooke-Lauder, J. (2008). Social change – Making the improbable possible through collaboration: NGOs working together in South Africa to tackle HIV/AIDS. Paper presented at *MOPAN Conference*, June, 2008.

Cornforth, C. (2001). Understanding the governance of non-profit organizations: Multiple perspectives and paradoxes. Draft paper prepared for the *Annual Conference of ARNOVA*, Miami, Florida, November 29-December 1, 2001.

Cummings, T. G. (1984). Trans-organizational development in research in organizational behaviour. *JAI Press*, 6, 367-422.

Dobrohoczki, R. (2008). Presentation Collaborative Governance Project - CUISR Internship Social Economy Workshop, May 2, 2008, Summer Internship Research Project with Saskatchewan Association for Community Living (SACL) and the Urban Aboriginal Strategy (UAS) in Saskatoon as part of the SSHRC sponsored project: *Linking, Learning, Leveraging Social Enterprises, Knowledgeable Economies*, Retrieved March 17, 2009 from www.caledoninst. org/Special_Projects/CG-COP/Docs/Workshop_presentation-collaborative_ governance.ppt

Doyle, M. E. & Smith, M. K. (2001). Shared leadership. *The Encyclopedia of Informal Education*. Retrieved January 2009 from http://www.infed.org/ leadership/shared_leadership.htm.

Drucker, P. (1992). *Managing the Non-Profit Organization: Practices and Principles*. Collins.

El Ansari, W. & Phillips, J. C. (2004). The costs and benefits to participants in community partnerships: A paradox in health promotion practice. *Society for Public Health Education*, 5(1), 35-48.

EL Ansari, W. E., Phillips, C. J., & Hammick, M. (2001). Collaboration and partnerships: Developing the evidence base. *Health and Social Care in the Community*, 9(4), 215.

Forbes, D. P. (1998). Measuring the unmeasurable: Empirical studies of nonprofit organizational effectiveness from 1977 to 1997. *Nonprofit and Volunteer Sector Quarterly*, 1998, 27(2), 183-202.

Franklin Dukes, E. & Solomon, M. (no date). *Reaching higher ground: A guide for preventing, preparing for, and transforming conflict for tobacco control coalitions*.Retrieved March 2009 from http://www.ttac.org/products/pdfs/ Higher_Ground.pdf.

Gloger, A. (2004). *The partnership-trustee journey: A handbook for community agencies in partnership*. East Scarborough Storefront.

Goleman, D. (1998). *Working with emotional intelligence*. New York: Bantam Dell Pub Group.

Greenleaf, R. (1977). *Servant leadership: A journey into the nature of legitimate power and greatness*. New York: Paulist Press.

Halford, S. (2004). Towards a sociology of organizational space. *Sociological Research Online*, 9(1). Retrieved from http://www.socresonline.org.uk/9/1/halford.html>

Hardy, C., Phillips, N. & Lawrence, T. B. (2003). Resources, knowledge and influence: The organizational effects of interorganizational collaboration. *Journal of Management Studies*, 40, 321-347.

Hittleman, M. (2008). *Discussion guide for community practitioners – Counting caring: attending to the human in an age of public management*. Retrieved July 24, 2008 from http://devsoc.cals.cornell.edu/cals/devsoc/outreach/cardi/publications/upload/counting-caring.pdf

Holcomb E. L. (2001). *Asking the right questions: Techniques for collaboration and school change*. Corwin Press.

Horn, R. E. (2001). Knowledge mapping for complex social messes. A presentation to the *Foundations in the Knowledge Economy* at the David and Lucile Packard Foundation, July 16, 2001. Retrieved February 2003 from http://stanford.edu/~rhorn/a/recent/spchKnwldgPACKARD.pdf

Herman, R. & Renz, D. (2008). *Nonprofit organizational effectiveness: Practical implications of research on an elusive concept*. Retrieved September 2008 from http://www.bsbpa.umkc.edu/mwcnl/research/RESEARCH.HTM.

Hittleman, M. (2007). *Counting caring: Attending to the human in an age of public management – A discussion guide for community practitioners*. Retrieved March 2009 from http://devsoc.cals.cornell.edu/cals/devsoc/outreach/cardi/publications/upload/counting-caring.pdf

Hudson, B., Hardy, B., Henwood, M., & Wistow, G. (1999). *In pursuit of inter-agency collaboration in the public sector: What is the contribution of theory and research?* UK: Nuffield Institute for Health.

Huxham, C. & Macdonald, D. (1992). Introducing collaborative advantage: Achieving inter-organizational effectiveness through meta-strategy. *Management Decision*, 30(3), p 50-56.

Impink, R.V. (1995). A case study of a nonprofit organization as a community coordination and integration mechanism for governmental and nonprofit organizations. In *Nonprofit organizations as public actors: Rising to new public policy challenges,* working papers. Washington DC: Independent Sector.

Innes, J. E. & Booher, D. E. (2003). *The impact of collaborative planning on governance capacity.* Center for Collaborative Policy. Retrieved July 2008 from http://repositories.cdlib.org/iurd/wps/WP-2003-03/

Jacobs, J. (1994). *Systems of survival: A dialogue on the moral foundations of commerce and politics.* Vintage Press.

Johnson, G. & Scholes, K.(2006). IBM global business services expanding the innovation horizon. *The Global CEO* Study 2006. Retrieved March 2007 from http://www-935.ibm.com/services/de/bcs/pdf/2006/ceostudy_engl.pdf

Kanigel, R. (2005). *The one best way: Frederick Winslow Taylor and the enigma of efficiency.* The MIT Press.

King, S. & Peterson, L. (2006). *Bridging boundaries: Lessons from leaders.* Starfield Consulting, Oakville, Ontario.

Kubisch, A. C., Fulbright-Anderson, K., & Connell, J. (1998). Evaluating community initiatives: A progress report. In K. Fulbright-Anderson, A. C. Kubisch, & J. P. Connell (Eds.), *New approaches to evaluating community initiatives: Theory, measurement, and analysis* (pp. 1-15). Washington, DC: The Aspen Institute.

Mattessich, P. W., Murray-Close, M., & Monsey, B. R. (2001). *Collaboration: What makes it work, 2nd edition.* St. Paul Amherst H. Wilder Foundation.

Martin, P. (2005). *A new kind of accountability.* Martin Training Associates, published on HR.com. Retrieved April 15, 2005 from http://www.hr.com/HRcom/index.cfm/74/92E9941D-9A08-4DFA-B5450214704B4B52?ost=rcFeature.

Mizrahi, T. & Rosenthal, B. B. (2001). Complexities of coalition building: Leaders' successes, strategies, struggles, and solutions. *Social Work,* 46(1), 63-78.

Morgan, G. (1996). *Images of organizations.* Sage Publications.

Murray, V. (2005). Prescriptive and research-based approaches to nonprofit boards: Linking parallel universes. Paper presented at the *Boards and Beyond Conference,* Midwest Center for Nonprofit Leadership, Kansas City, Missouri,

Spring 2005. Retrieved August 2009 from http://www.bloch.umkc.edu/mwcnl/
Conferences/GovernanceConf2005/Post%20Conference%20Materials.pdf

New Economy Development Group (2005). *Trends in collaboration: Lessons
learned from sectoral involvement in departmental policy development*
(SIDPD) and beyond. Voluntary Sector Forum. Retrieved October 2008 from
http://www.vsi-isbc.org/eng/policy/pdf/sidpd_final_report.pdf

Ostrower, F. (2005). The reality underneath the buzz of partnerships: The
potentials and pitfalls of partnering. *Stanford Social Innovation Review*, Spring,
34-41.

Patton, Michael Quinn. (1996). *Utilization-focused evaluation: The new century
text, third edition*. Sage Publications Inc.

Phillips, S. D. (2004). The myths of horizontal governance: Is the third sector
really a partner? Paper presented to the *International Society for Third-Sector
Research (ISTR) Conference*, Toronto, July 2004. Retrieved July 2008 from
http://www.istr.org/conferences/toronto/workingpapers/phillips.susan.pdf

Reeler D. (no date provided). *A theory of social change and implications for
practice, planning, monitoring and evaluation*. Community Development
Resource Association. Retrieved July 15 2008 from http://www.cdra.org.za/
articles/ATheoryofSocialChangebyDougReeler.pdf

Renz, D. O. (2006). Reframing governance, transcending the organization. *Non
Profit Quarterly*, 1(4), xp6-13

Roberts, J. (2004). *Alliances, coalitions and partnerships: Building collaborative
organizations*. New Society Publishers.

Roberts, J. & O'Connor, P. (2008). Inter-agency services collaboration: Does it
exist? Does it work? Is it worth it? Article presented at the *15th International
conference on multi-organizational Partnerships, Alliances and Networks*,
MOPAN, 25–27 June 2008, Boston, MA.

Rubin, H. (1998). *Collaboration Skills for Educators and Nonprofit Leaders*.
Chicago: Lyceum Books.

Saidel, J. R. (1998). Expanding the governance construct: Functions and
contributions of nonprofit advisory groups. *Nonprofit and Voluntary Sector
Quarterly*, 27(4), 421-436.

Schutz, W. C. (1958). FIRO: *A three-dimensional theory of interpersonal
behavior*. New York: Rinehart, & Winston.

Shortell, S. M., Gillies, R. R., Anderson, D. A., Morgan-Erickson, K., & Mitchell, J. B. (2000). Integrating health care delivery. *Health Forum Journal*, (Nov/ Dec), 35 39.

Spady, R. J., Bell, Jr., C. H., D'Angelo, G. A. (1995). *A new view of authority and the administrative process*. Retrieved April 2008 from http://www. forumfoundation.org/newview.

Stone, M. M. (1996). Competing contexts: The evolution of a nonprofit organization's governance system in multiple environments. *Administration and Society*, 28(1), 61-89.

Takashi, L. (2002). Collaborative windows and organizational governance: Exploring the formation and demise of social service partnerships. *Nonprofit and Voluntary Sector Quarterly*, 31(2), 165-185.

Takahashi, L. M. & Smutny, G. (2001). Collaboration among small community-based organizations: Strategies and challenges in turbulent environments. *Journal of Planning Education and Research*, 21, 141-153.

Taylor-Powell, E., Rossing, B., & Geran, J. (1998). *Evaluating collaboratives: Reaching the potential*. Retrieved from http://cf.uwex.edu/ces/pubs/pdf/ G3658_8.pdf

Vollmer, C. (2009). Digital Darwinism. In *Strategy+business Electronic Newsletter*. Booz & Company.

Waddell, S. (2005). *Social integration: A global societal learning and change perspective*. A presentation to the United Nations Department of Economic and Social Affairs Expert Group Meeting on Dialogue in the Social Integration Process. New York. Downloaded from http://www.instituteforstrategicclarity. org/Publications/SocialIntegrationSteveWaddell.doc

Walsh, P., McGregor-Lowndes, M., & Newton, C. (2006). *Shared services: Lessons from the public and private sectors for the nonprofit sector*. CPNS Working Paper No 34. Nonprofit Standard Chart of Accounts (Queensland University of Technology), Brisbane: QLD. Retrieved from http://eprints.qut. edu.au.

Weiner, B. J. & Alexander, J. A. (1998). The challenges of governing public-private community health partnerships. *Health Care Management Review*, 23(2), 39-55.

World Commission on Environment and Development. (1987). Our common future, Report of the World Commission on Environment and Development. Published as Annex to General Assembly document A/42/427, Development and International Co-operation: Environment August 2, 1987.

Interagency Services Collaboration Project Reports
Banasiak, K. (2007). *Policy supports to the NPO sector: A quick scan of other jurisdictions.* Wellesley Institute.

Boutillier, M., O'Connor, P., Zizys, T., Roberts, J., & Banasiak, K. (2007) *Does collaborative service delivery improve client and organization outcomes? A review of the evidence on NPO collaboration in health and social services.* Wellesley Institute.

Graham, H. (2007). *The state of service delivery collaboration in the Toronto NPO sector: A key informant study.* Wellesley Institute.

Horwath, R. (2007). *Service delivery collaboration in nonprofit health and community services: What does government want?* Wellesley Institute.

Roberts, J. (2007). *Revisioning KIN: A service delivery system visioning project.* Wellesley Institute.

Roberts, J. & Banasiak, K. (2007). *Proceedings from a roundtable held on October 11, 2007, Toronto, Canada.* Wellesley Institute.

Roberts, J. & O'Connor, P. (2007). *Inter-agency service collaboration in the NPO sector - Report overview.* Wellesley Institute.

Roche, B. & Roberts, J. (2007). *The East Scarborough Storefront Project: A successful inter-organizational service collaboration.* Wellesley Institute.

Zizys, T. (2007). *Collaboration within business and government: What are the objectives, and what is achieved? A scan of the evidence.* Wellesley Institute.

Download the Wellesley Institute reports at www.joanroberts.com.

Appendix A
Sample Organizational Collaboration Policy
ABC NON-PROFIT Collaboration Policy

To further of its mission, ABC NON-PROFIT may enter into collaborations with non-profit or for-profit entities.

Definition of Collaboration

For purposes of this policy, a collaboration refers to any contractual agreement between ABC NON-PROFIT and another entity under which ABC NON-PROFIT and one or more partners share financial profits and losses of a mutual undertaking or undertake joint activities which require a formalized commitment.

Identification of Collaboration Opportunities

It shall be the responsibility of the Executive Director to identify collaboration opportunities for ABC NON-PROFIT that will assist the organization in accomplishing its mission more efficiently or effectively. The Executive Director shall report to the Board of Directors from time to time on his/her efforts to identify and develop collaboration opportunities.

Evaluation of Collaboration Opportunities

ABC NON-PROFIT shall enter into a collaboration only if the collaboration relates directly to the interest of the organization and furthers the organization's mission in a way that the Organization could not accomplish on its own.

Authority of Approve Collaborations

The ABC NON-PROFIT Board of Directors shall have final authority to approve all collaboration agreements.

Mandatory Terms in Collaboration Agreements

ABC NON-PROFIT will enter into a collaboration only if the binding collaboration documents:

* Permit use of ABC NON-PROFIT's name and logo only by parties to the agreement and only in connection with the specific activities of the collaboration.

* Specifies expectations for the organization's participation with respect to decision-making, assignment of staff to programs and projects, and any financial resources to be incurred from jointly managed activities.

* Indemnify the association for losses arising out of actions by the partner organization.

* Contain explicit termination clauses.

* Indicate the degree to which the collaboration is an exclusive agreement.

Appendix B
Sample Terms of Reference for a Collaborative Steering Committee

1. A collaborative steering committee/group is hereby established to be known as *(name of group)*.

2. The following constitutes the terms of reference of *(name of steering committee/ group)*.

3. In these terms of reference *(abbreviation for steering committee/group)* refers to *(state full name of steering committee/group)*.

Membership

4. Membership of the committee/group will comprise the following organisations/ individuals: *List membership organisations/individuals*

5. Other organisations/groups/individuals that may have an interest in the development of (name of committee/group) may be invited to join the committee/group at any time with the agreement of the listed members.

6. The membership of the committee shall be restricted to two representatives per organisation, one of which should be drawn from the Board.

Meetings

7. Meetings will be held at regular intervals but not less than once a month. To be properly constituted, a quorum is required of 50% of members.

8. The venue for each meeting will be decided by the committee/group and will, in as far as possible, be reflective of the membership of the committee/group and the geographical remit of the planned service. (A suitable central venue might be used or venues might be changed to reflect full geographic spread.)

Decision-making

9. Decisions will be made through consensus. In the event of unresolved conflict, (conversation lasts more than an hour), a supermajority vote of 75% will be taken.

Chair

10. Each meeting will be led by the chairperson chosen at the first meeting. The Chair will facilitate meetings to ensure buy-in from all involved.

Records

11. A record of each meeting will be kept by a designated note-taker. Note taking will revolve to each member of the committee/group. It is the responsibility of the designated note-taker to ensure that each member of the committee/group receives the notes from the previous meeting not less than 24 hours before the

date of the next meeting. (Alternatively, a secretary may be appointed at the first meeting.)

Purpose

12. The purpose of the *(collaborative/group)* is to facilitate and oversee the development of a the *(name of project)* through advocacy and program development and in doing so to:

- Address the strategic issues involved in establishing the (name) including but not limited to:

  - The aims and objectives of the *(name of project)*

  - The timing and resources needed to roll-out the *(name of project)*

  - The structure of the *(name)* *(including type of legal entity, management structure, etc)*

- Source and apply for funding for the development of the *(name of project)*.

13. Amendments to these Terms of Reference may be made at any time with the agreement of the committee.

Timeframe

14. The (steering committee/group) will review its purpose, aims, objectives, and achievements to date six (6) months after the date of formation of the collaborative.

Appendix C
A Sample Format for Policy Development

- Definition of issue, rationale, or need for policy

- Preamble or broad policy statement

- Purpose and goals

- Policy guidelines or principles

- Proposed program including its application, scope, and resource implications

- Responsibilities of staff and others board/employees, depending on policy and existing administrative capacity

- Mechanisms for review

Appendix D
Sample Communications Policy: For the ABC Health Promotion Collaborative

Need for Policy:
ABC Health Promotion collaborative is involved in the work of promoting health in the local community of Anytown. A communications policy is needed to ensure effective communication of our health messages to the target population of Anytown and surrounding areas.

Preamble or Broad Policy Statement:
It is the intent of the ABC collaborative to communicate effectively and frequently with the population of Anytown and surrounding areas. In order to communicate effectively, this document is intended to act as policy and procedural guideline for members of the collaborative.

Purpose and Goals:
The purpose of ABC Health Promotion Collaborative is to promote a healthy community and raise public awareness of our health issue.

Our goals are:
• To raise awareness and educate the human service delivery system about our health issue

• To raise awareness of the issue and identify resources for those at risk of our health issue

• To educate the broader public and reduce the stigma associated with our health issue

Policy Guidelines or Principles:
The ABC Health Promotion Collaborative shall communicate on a regular basis with all those who are interested in supporting our goals and objectives, including representatives of all levels of government, other community-based organizations, corporations, foundations, and members of the community at large.

Communication mechanisms will include a website, quarterly newsletter, frequent press releases, public meetings, and flyers to promote special events.

Communications materials will include a contact name and phone number, an agenda where possible, and an invitation to participate in ABC Health Promotion Collaborative events. Communication material will include a feedback mechanism wherever possible.

ABC Health Promotion Collaborative will always have at least two designated spokespersons for media enquiries, one automatically being the chairperson of the collaborative.

All meetings of the collaborative are open to the public, although the committee may go in camera to deal with personnel, real estate, or litigation matters.

Members of the public may address the ABC Health Promotion Collaborative by contacting the Chair and/ or Coordinator.

As members of the ABC Health Promotion Collaborative may from time to time have conflicting perspectives on the content of key messages, any new key messages developed for any event or channel of communication must be distributed electronically to all members of the collaborative for review and feedback. If there is no reaction within five days of electronic distribution, the initiating group can proceed with their plans. In the event of disputed wording, the collaborative members will attempt to work out compromise language via electronic communication. If this fails, a members meeting will be called to resolve the issue.

Proposed Program Including its Application and Scope and Resource Implications:
A communications program will consist of a part-time communications coordinator and an annual itemized budget, which includes line items for communication channels including a website and print brochures.

Communication projects will be itemized in the annual budget and approved by the governing body.

Responsibilities of Staff and Other Board/Employees, Depending on Policy and Existing Administrative Capacity:
This communications policy will be enacted by all staff employed by the collaborative or seconded to it and members of the collaborative decision-making body.

Mechanisms for Review:
This policy will be reviewed by the governing body of the ABC Health Promotion Collaborative on a bi-annual basis.

Appendix E

Tool to Create a Memorandum of Understanding for a Collaborative Agreement

An effective Memorandum of Understanding (or MOU) prevents

misunderstandings and disputes by clarifying the expectations of the partners. The process of developing an MOU is an instructive and potentially invaluable experience in collaborating. By asking for the information needed to complete the MOU, you will learn how responsive your partner/s will be. You may also learn how your partner deals with conflict.

These documents typically contain the following:

- Background or a brief description of the project

- The specific activities that each partner will perform (e.g., specific services to be delivered, activities associated with participation in the partnership)

- Other agreements related to how the partners will work together, communication methods, division of authority, etc.

- Length of the agreement and/or timeline

- Whether your partners have liability and other types of insurance

- What the partners are specifically willing to promise (ambitious projections may dissipate as your partner commits to something realistic)

- What aspects of the project is each member responsible for

- The collaborative member's overall commitment to the project

Any refusal to put anything in writing is a red flag and may be the sole reason not to proceed with the arrangement.

A number of elements should be included in a typical Memorandum of Understanding. Since each project and its partners are unique, the following suggestions are provided as an example.

Project Purpose:
Start off with some background or a brief description of the project. Answer the question of why you are collaborating and what you hope to achieve.

Members of the Collaborative Who Will Sign the Agreement:
Identify the organizations that are members of the collaborative and who will sign the document on the organization's behalf.

The Period:
Specify a time period for the collaboration. Usually the agreement timeframe will

follow a funding cycle.

Assignments/Responsibilities:
This important section of the agreement describes the duties and responsibilities of each partner. Identify programming, managerial, and governance responsibilities. The number one purpose of a written agreement is to clarifying responsibilities.

Conflict Resolution:
Include a simple process for how conflict will be resolved. If your decision-making process breaks down, for example with a tie vote, or if your group is in conflict, identify a process you can use for resolution. Dispute resolution services are often provided by non-profits or law schools. Refer to pre-existing governance documents such as roles and responsibilities and polices to identify decision-making and communication processes.

Staffing:
In collaboratives with staff, be clear who the employer is. Is the collaborative the employer or a trustee? Then identify the day-to-day decisions that are delegated to employees and provide clear parameters on staff decision-making. Some of the kinds of decisions you may need to make include identifying who has the authority to spend money on behalf of the collaborative, who makes hiring decisions and decisions about policy or the direction that your program will take, and how to make decisions to apply for grants.

Disclaimers:
Many MOUs contain one or more disclaimers, including one indicating that employees of Organization A are not to be considered employees, borrowed or otherwise, of Organization B and vice versa. It may also be worthwhile to disclaim what the collaboration is not intended to do, guarantee, or create.

Financial Arrangements:
A typical collaboration will have financial implications. These should be spelled out in detail, including which entity will pay for each item and when payment is due. In the event of funding from an outside funder, identify who will receive and manage the funding. Be clear on how the collaborative's funds will be managed either by a trustee or the collaborative itself.

Risk Sharing:
Another critical element of an MOU is a description of who will bear the risk of a mishap. What if something goes wrong? What if the collaboration's activities result in injury, death or a financial loss?

Insurance Requirements:
This section indicates the insurance requirements that each organization places on the other. In some cases, one organization will require that its partner/s have certain insurance in place.

Be sure to review any legal agreements with a lawyer prior to execution.

Appendix F

RASCI Model
The RASCI model is a tool to assign responsibility when planning a project to ensure the assignments are carried out. It is particularly useful when developing the communications strategy for major change initiative.

The RASCI model specifies the following:

• Responsible: the person responsible for implementing the task in the project plan

• Accountable: the person to whom "R" is Accountable and is the authority who approves to sign-off on work before it is effective

• Supportive: the person who provides resources or plays a supporting role in implementation

• Consulted: the persons that can provide information and/or expertise to help move the project forward

• Informed: the persons who need to be notified of results but need not necessarily be consulted

RASCI chart:

TASK	RESPONSIBLE	ACCOUNTABLE	SUPPORTIVE	CONSULTED	INFORMED

5468862R0

Made in the USA
Charleston, SC
19 June 2010